RHINESTONES
AND
TWANGING TONES

RHINESTONES
AND
TWANGING TONES

The Look and Sound of
Country Music

Mac Yasuda and Jim Washburn

Published in 2018 by Hal Leonard Books
An Imprint of Hal Leonard LLC
7777 West Bluemound Road
Milwaukee, WI 53213

Trade Book Division Editorial Offices
33 Plymouth St., Montclair, NJ 07042

Printed in the United States of America

Book design by Damien Castaneda

Library of Congress Cataloging-in-Publication Data

Names: Yasuda, Mac, author. | Washburn, Jim, 1955- author.
Title: Rhinestones and twanging tones : the look and sound of country music /
   Mac Yasuda and Jim Washburn.
Description: Montclair, NJ : Hal Leonard Books, 2018.
Identifiers: LCCN 2017029941 | ISBN 9781495088131 (hardcover)
Subjects: LCSH: Guitars--Pictorial works. | Yasuda, Mac--Musical instrument
   collections--Pictorial works. | Guitar--Collectors and collecting. |
   Country musicians--Portraits. | Cohn, Nudie, 1902-1984.
Classification: LCC ML1015.G9 Y37 2017 | DDC 781.642075--dc23
LC record available at https://lccn.loc.gov/2017029941

www.halleonardbooks.com

Contents

Foreword

I first met Mac Yasuda in 1970, very shortly after I opened my shop in Nashville. At that time, Mac was an aspiring young player eager to learn about American music and guitars. Since then, my business has expanded from a 1,200-square-foot first location to an 18,000-square-foot building with three floors full of guitars. Mac has become known for having amassed one of the world's finest collections of vintage American guitars, banjos, and country music memorabilia, including a very extensive collection of celebrity-owned stage clothing by Nudie and others.

When I visited Japan in 1974, there were already three Japanese magazines devoted to bluegrass music, and a number of music stores in major cities such as Tokyo, Osaka, and Kobe that featured vintage as well as new American instruments. I have fond memories of my visit with Mac at his mountaintop home in Kobe at that time. During the 1970s, Mac, as well as a number of other collectors and dealers in Japan, became some of my best customers and close friends. The Japanese economy was very strong and Japanese interest in American music was very strong. Japanese and European collectors had a profound impact on the market for vintage American fretted instruments. Since prices, to a very large extent, are determined by supply versus demand, when interest in vintage instruments was very high in Japan and Western Europe, and their economies were growing rapidly, prices of American vintage fretted instruments were just as often determined by how much collectors were willing to pay in Tokyo, London, or Dusseldorf as by how much American buyers were willing to pay. Many of the finest vintage American fretted instruments and country music memorabilia items flowed from the USA to Japan and Europe, but over the years, and especially from 1985 through 2000, Japanese demand was a strong market driver.

Throughout all of this period, Mac Yasuda was a central figure in the Japanese market and became very well known to collectors and dealers worldwide.

In addition to the impact of their spending on vintage instruments, Japanese collectors were some of the most meticulous historical researchers. The information published in a variety of Japanese magazines covering vintage American fretted instruments was more detailed and extensive than in virtually any American publications of the 1970s through the 1990s.

Over the years Mac Yasuda has been a meticulous researcher, avid collector, and a personal friend of many musicians. During a recent visit to his home in Newport Beach, California, I was highly impressed by his collection of instruments and memorabilia and his profound passion and deep respect for the craftsmen and musicians whose work he has collected, and the acquaintances he has made over the years. *Rhinestones and Twanging Tones* features great photos of important instruments and memorabilia, as well as highly informative and enjoyable reading.

—George Gruhn

Acknowledgments

Jim Washburn would like to thank, first off, the Fullerton Museum Center in Fullerton, California, and its staff for hosting Mac and my "Rhinestones and Twangin' Tones" exhibit in 2006. Thanks to the following folks for being so generous with their help and advice: Jamie Nudie of Nudie's Rodeo Tailors, musician/historian Deke Dickerson, guitar repairman/historian Steve Soest, Ren Wall of Heritage Guitars, Richard Johnston of Gryphon Stringed Instruments, and the indispensable Dick Boak at C. F. Martin & Co. My thanks to Mac Yasuda, who was a tireless pleasure to work with on this book. Along with bothering to own most of this stuff, he took nearly every photo in the book. Thanks to my wife Leslie Smith (who helped edit the photos) and the rest of my family and friends for putting up with my pouty writing process. And thanks to Lindsay Wagner, our editor at Hal Leonard, as well as copy editor James Barnett and designer Damien Castaneda for their efforts.

Mac Yasuda would like to thank my wife, Kimiyo, and children Ken, Sotaro, Naohisa, and Mami, as well as my parents and brothers for the efforts they made so I could come to America. Thanks as well to my fiddler friend of a half-century, Hiroshi Yasuhara. I'm eternally grateful to my schoolmate Masao Okkotsu for introducing me to country music, and to George Gruhn for teaching me so much about them. I am grateful to the Grand Ole Opry musicians and staff for making me so welcome there, and to Norman Harris, Larry Briggs, and the rest of the vintage guitar community. Jim Washburn and his wife Leslie were fine companions on the journey of doing this book. My thanks to all my musician friends—especially Norman Blake and Marty Stuart—as well as Billy Walker, Hank Snow, Porter Wagoner, and the many others now in Hillbilly Heaven.

Introduction

This book is about the threads and strings that bind country music together, specifically the fanciful clothing and guitars that helped define the look and sound of country in its classic days, when it was direct, wide-awake music that spoke to the dreams and hardscrabble lives of its fans. It was the sound of tradition that actually invented its traditions as it went along.

This is also a book about love and obsession, about the effect country music had on a teenager who grew up half a world away from the country that country music sang about. Nearly every object depicted on these pages was collected by Japan-born Mac Yasuda over several decades. It is perhaps the largest collection of country music equipage that is not yet locked behind glass in a museum, and it is the direct consequence of Mac's hearing a four-song Hank Snow record half a century ago.

THE MUSIC

Was there ever music with a greater sense of place than country and western? The name alone is a sure giveaway, as are its subgenres bluegrass, western swing, the Nashville Sound, the Bakersfield Sound, and other titles that speak of tilled earth, saddle sores, and crude oil. It's the sort of music you'd sing into a bar of Lava soap as you washed away the grime of the day. It is the plainspoken song of the people of the heartland, a music steeped in authenticity and rooted to the ground it sprang from.

Except, of course, for the Alpine yodeling, and the Hawaiian guitars, and the lyrics tracing back to Scottish murder ballads and Celtic fiddle reels, and song structures and vocal filigrees based on African-American blues, or tunes created by professional songsmiths to be sung around fake campfires on Hollywood soundstages.

◁ The headstock of Hank Snow's famed Martin D-45 guitar, backed with one of his many Nudie suits. Earlier clothiers may have had a fanciful vision of western wear, but Nudie Cohn's creations were a delirious Hollywood dream of rustic American life, swirling in color and eye-riveting rhinestones. As singer Bill Anderson once said of Nudie suits, "Anything worth doing is worth overdoing." And while Nudie's rhinestones were scratching up the backs of their guitars, Snow and other country artists liked their instruments to show a bit of flash as well.

⬔ **On the frontier, music often took a back seat to other forms of entertainment, as depicted in an image from the 1836 edition of Davy Crockett's Almanack.**

That's not to say the country music of old can't ring as pure and true as a bell made of alloyed metals. It's just that things aren't as simple as they might seem.

Musicologists have indeed traced some country melodies and lyrics back hundreds of years to British Isles origins, passed down largely intact through generations of oral history of the Scots-Irish immigrants who settled in the Appalachian South.

Yodeling, meanwhile, had been a minor fad in the US since it was introduced by touring Tyrolean troupes in the 1840s. (Another wave of European entertainers in the 1880s popularized the mandolin, later adopted by bluegrass musicians.)

Yodeling was popular enough that it became one of the styles adapted into minstrel shows, in which both white and black entertainers donned crude "blackface" makeup, apparently affording them license to emote more freely than the strictures of Eurocentric culture allowed.

When phonograph records came along, ethnic music sold well in the new medium, and yodeling was featured on Thomas Edison's wax cylinders as early as 1892, thirty-two years before Riley Puckett yodeled on a country record.

Early blues music had a major influence on country. (The influence flowed both ways: Howlin' Wolf said he arrived at his signature moan as a retort to Jimmie Rodgers' yodeling.) Some artists heard blues music on recordings, or via the white interpretations of the influential blackface singer Emmett Miller, or directly from the porches of their African-American sharecropping neighbors.

The steel guitar originated in Hawaii in the late 1800s when someone figured out a guitar's pitch could be determined with a metal bar slid over the strings. The steel guitar and ukulele became sensations in the States after Hawaiian musicians were showcased at 1915's Panama-Pacific International Exposition in San Francisco.

Ukes never made much of an inroad with country music, but the cry of the steel guitar became a staple in the 1920s. When the success of Jimmie Rodgers' records codified the sound of country music late in that decade, the steel guitar was a prominent part, as were yodeling and blues music.

A former railroad man with a life-worn voice, Rodgers was billed as "the Singing Brakeman," and often appeared in his work overalls and cap. Others had to stretch a bit to create their legends. The singer Montana Slim, for example, was born Wilfred Carter in Nova Scotia, performed on British cruise liners, and was dubbed "Montana Slim" while residing and doing a radio show in New York City. Singing cowboy Tex Fletcher was a NYC native, who was born Geremino Bisceglia.

Many of the singing cowboys sported guitars that would never fit in a horse's overhead compartment. The guitars the cowboys of old had were scarce and small, "parlor size" instruments strung with gut strings. Gene Autry, meanwhile, appeared in westerns with the first Martin D-45, a steel-stringed Dreadnought guitar (named for the largest warship) so large that even its manufacturer was wary of it. (Letters exist of company head C.F Martin III actually discouraging customers from buying Dreadnoughts.)

Country musicians were also quick to embrace innovations such as resonator guitars—where the string's volume was boosted by a spun-aluminum cone—and electric guitars once they came along. Leo Fender's radical solidbody guitars have fueled rock and roll for over sixty years, but he originally developed them with country pickers in mind.

INTRODUCTION

THE CLOTHING

Cowboys had been mythologized since the dime novels and Wild West shows of the late 1800s, and they were popular fodder for early movies as well. The advent of motion picture sound inspired Hollywood to invent the singing cowboy: a heroic figure who fought villains and serenaded cattle and townswomen with his voice and guitar, while wearing spotless, fanciful outfits that were just waiting for color film to do them justice.

On actual cattle drives, cowboys were far more likely to curse their cattle than to sing to them, and they wore whatever clothing they could afford or stitch together. Buckskins were typically tanned with a mash made of deer brains, which didn't smell the least bit romantic. Denim didn't fare much better after unwashed months in the saddle.

Early country and western outfitters Nathan Turk of Van Nuys, California, and Bernard "Rodeo Ben" Lichenstein of Philadelphia, Pennsylvania, were both Polish immigrants, and drew upon Eastern European folk costume designs, from understated piping at the pockets and collars up to florid embroidery never worn in the West of yore.

It took Nudie Cohn, though, to make western wear into the stuff of dreams.

Born Nuta Kotlyarenko in Kiev, Ukraine, in 1902, family lore has it that Nudie was already in love with cowboy movies before he immigrated to America at the age of eleven, sent along with his brother to escape the pogroms of Eastern Europe. Relatives in the States had already shortened the family name to Cohn, and an Ellis Island clerk—perhaps inclined towards practical jokes—changed Nuta's first name to "Nudie."

Nudie had apprenticed to a tailor in Kiev when he was eight. A tailor is what he became in the US, after first scuffling to make a living, crisscrossing the country, trying everything from boxing to film editing. He

⚠ **A family of homesteaders on the Western plains in the 1880s. Note the absence of rhinestones and Hawaiian guitars.**

⚠ **Nudie Cohn, in the saddle of one of the eighteen cars he westernized. He would take a Pontiac or Cadillac and customize it with steer horns, tooled leather, pearl-handled revolvers, and hundreds of silver dollars.**

wound up back in New York, making rhinestone-bedecked outfits for strippers and burlesque dancers.

When he and his wife Bobbie moved to Los Angeles, he applied the skills learned on undergarments to making western wear. His first customer was singer Tex Williams (from Illinois, of course), who auctioned a horse to give Nudie the money to buy a new sewing machine. A young Hank Thompson saw Williams' suit and bought one for himself. Business snowballed from there. Before long, Nudie was outfitting many of the West Coast country singers, cowboy movie stars, and western swing bands. That latter style

of music—to further confuse country music's pedigree—owed as much to the Gypsy jazz of Django Reinhardt's Hot Club of Paris as it did to the honky-tonks of Abilene.

Before long, Nashville was also under Nudie's spangled thrall. To prime the pump, Nudie tracked down Porter Wagoner near the start of his success and made him a suit for free. Wagoner subsequently bought and wore over fifty suits, and his tall, lanky frame became a walking billboard for Nudie's works. Hank Snow and other Nashville giants also had closet poles sagging under the weight of their many Nudie suits.

⌂ Saddle leather, but no horse. Singer Webb Pierce with his custom Nudiemobile. The image projected by country stars and singing cowboys was a world removed from the sweat, grime, and functional clothing real cowboys lived with.

▷ Nudie in his element, playing his mandolin onstage in the 1970s at the Palomino, Southern California's longtime honky-tonk palace.

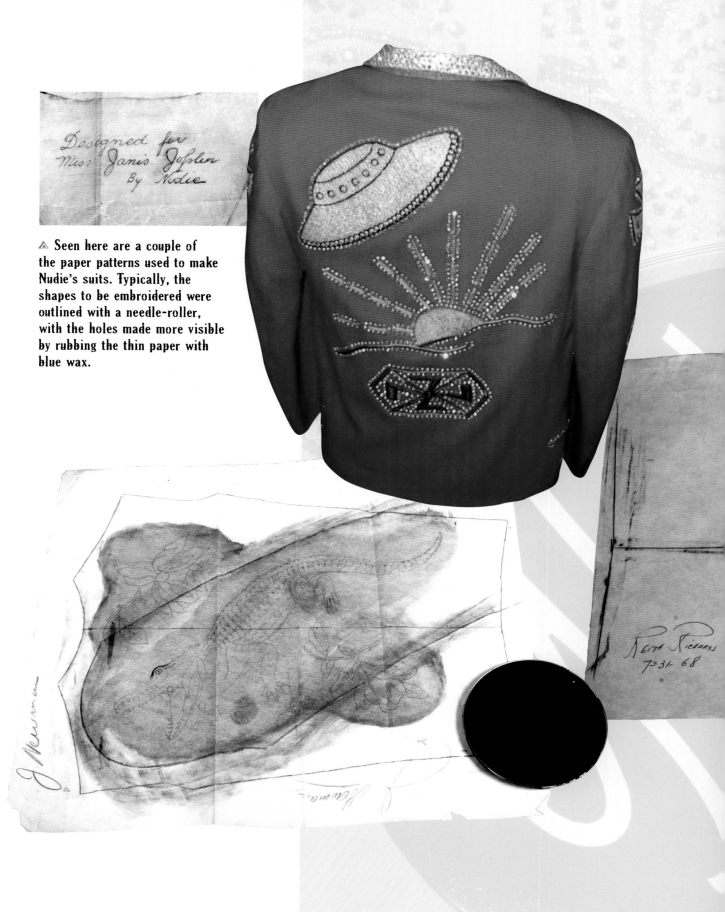

Designed for Miss Janis Joplin By Nudie

△ Seen here are a couple of the paper patterns used to make Nudie's suits. Typically, the shapes to be embroidered were outlined with a needle-roller, with the holes made more visible by rubbing the thin paper with blue wax.

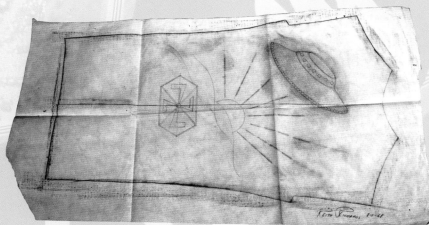

◁ In the late **1960**s, musicians who had grown weary of psychedelia turned to a hybrid of country and rock. Nudie was only too glad to clothe them as well. Country-rock fulcrum Gram Parsons of the Flying Burrito Brothers brought in his friend Keith Richards to get a suit. Here are two of the paper pattern pieces and the result.

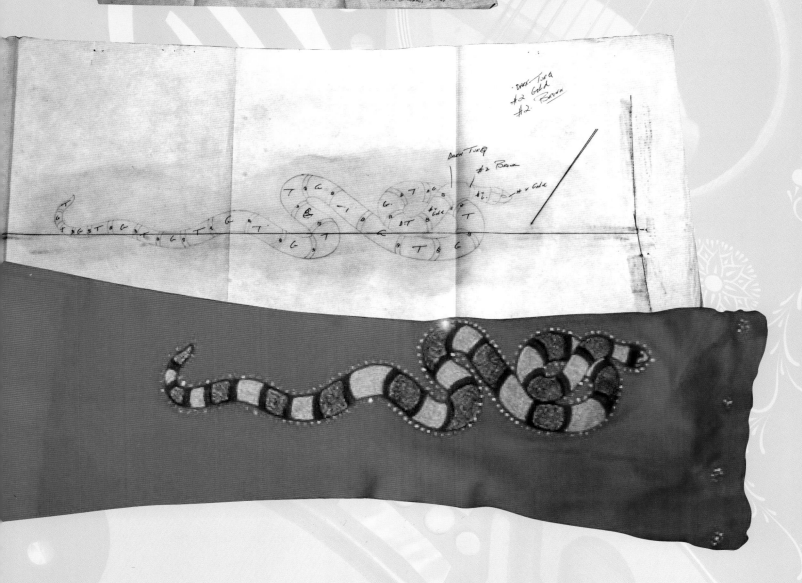

THE FAN

So there you have country: the music of heartland America made from an international smorgasbord of sounds, and attired like a fevered combination of Hollywood cowboys and New York strippers. What better to represent a nation of immigrants and dreamers?

The music certainly hit home with millions of listeners. People whose lives had blown away in the Dust Bowl held onto their Jimmie Rodgers 78s, because his songs helped them feel less lost. Hank Snow once received a letter from a family whose mother had drawn so much sustenance from his music that she'd directed that she be buried with a photo of him in her casket.

And country didn't just reach American hearts. Fans in Soviet Estonia would get Johnny Cash 45s smuggled in from Finland. When Nigerian bandleader King Sunny Adé and his African Beats became a world music sensation in the 1980s, fans wondered how the hell a pedal steel guitar wound up in his band. Adé, like many Nigerians, it turned out, was a huge fan of Jim Reeves' smooth voice and Nashville arrangements.

And in 1964, fifteen-year-old Makoto Yasuda

⚠ **Young country fan Mac Yasuda, at home near Kobe, Japan, a long way from the Grand Ole Opry.**

⚠ **An audience photo of Hank Snow performing in Kobe, Japan, in 1967. That fuzzy silhouette in the foreground is Mac Yasuda, in the first row.**

was enjoying a normal teenaged life near Kobe, Japan, when a friend showed up with an EP record of four Hank Snow songs, with a cover photo showing Snow aglow in a pink Nudie suit.

"I thought it was the best thing I'd ever heard. The honesty and directness in his voice got right to me. When the Beatles came along, it was too late. I was already in love with country music," Mac says.

He and his friend bought pawnshop guitars and put a country band together, including a violin player from the school orchestra who had never heard country music. Mac and the others were only a step or two ahead of that. The only books of "country" sheet music they could find had

songs like "Old MacDonald." Country was hardly played on the radio, and there were no books or magazines about it.

Mac and his friends couldn't figure out why their nylon-stringed guitars sounded nothing like the robust cannons they heard on records. Japan had a long history of classical guitar making, and had jumped into the budget electric market, but steel-string acoustic guitars were almost unknown.

Mac and his compatriots decided the difference must be the pickguards they saw on the guitars shown on album covers. So they bought sheets of black plastic, cut them to shape, glued them to their classical guitars, and wondered why they still didn't sound right.

By 1967, the Japanese were making a few decent steel-string guitars, and Mac and his band were playing them at stage shows and radio appearances.

Hank Snow toured Japan that year, and when he played in Kobe, Mac and his bandmates were in the first row. Mac was bowled over by the music, and dazzled when the stage lights hit the rhinestones on Snow's red Nudie suit.

"I'd seen record covers where he was wearing one, but that was nothing like the way it sparkled in person. It was so exotic and fancy, but it seemed to fit with the music, like they belonged together. I had no idea what a Nudie suit was, but I wanted one."

During the show, they handed Snow an assemblage of 1,000 origami cranes they had made to honor him, and were invited to meet him backstage.

In the concert, Snow had played a worn 1934 Martin D-28, which baffled Mac.

"He was a very successful guy, and could afford anything. I asked him, 'Why don't you play a shiny new guitar like mine?'

"He laughed at that, and his whole band did, too, and he said, 'Kid, you don't know nothing about guitars.'"

Properly chagrined, Mac made sure he'd learned a bit about old guitars by the time he came

▲ **The fateful Hank Snow EP a friend brought to Mac Yasuda's attention.**

⚠ **Mac Yasuda and his high school country band. Mac's guitar is a Hotaka, the first playable Japanese copy of a Martin Dreadnought. That's Hank Snow and the Rainbow Ranch Boys' autographs on it, from the night Mac got schooled about "old" guitars. The other guitarist is Mac's friend Masao, who introduced him to Hank Snow's music.**

to the US in 1970 on an engineering scholarship to Michigan Tech. Near the end of the school year, he managed to get himself sent to a student conference in Nashville, and blew off the conference to hit the town. He sang with a couple of bar bands, dropped in at RCA (where Chet Atkins graciously showed Mac around the studio), visited with Hank Snow at his house, and made a pilgrimage to GTR, the fledgling guitar shop George Gruhn had with Tut Taylor and Randy Wood.

He saw one of his dream guitars there, a Gibson SJ-200 like Porter Wagoner played. It was $450, and he only had $25. He recalls, "I swore then that someday I'd have *all* the SJ-200s."

He's not there yet, but it's not for want of trying. Mac began dealing in vintage guitars, becoming a respected expert and collector of them, which put him in touch with many of his musical idols, some of whom became his friends. Whenever he could, he'd collect and preserve the musical gear and clothing they'd made famous.

Mac wound up performing on the Grand Ole Opry dozens of times, and generally living a life that he never would have even dreamed of had he not heard Hank Snow's voice calling out from a seven-inch record in his youth.

More on that later. We have some guitars and spangled suits to meet.

RHINESTONES
AND
TWANGING
TONES

Chapter I

The Sons of the Pioneers

The Sons of the Pioneers epitomized the vocal group sound on the western side of country and western, with their rich harmonies on songs like "Cool Water" and "Tumbling Tumbleweeds" evoking an idealized version of the cowboy life.

The group got its start in Hollywood in 1931 when Cincinnati-born Leonard Slye started a duo with Bob Nolan, a Canadian who had been living on the beach. It eventually expanded to five members, including Texas-born brothers Karl and Hugh Farr. Both were fine singers, while Karl's guitar and Hugh's fiddle added a western swing and Gypsy jazz lilt to the proceedings.

Slye left the group in 1937 to try a solo career in acting. The following year, he was signed by Republic Pictures to take Gene Autry's place in a western after Autry went on strike. The studio changed Slye's name to Roy Rogers, and he went on to equal Autry's fame as a screen cowboy.

The Sons of the Pioneers were along for much of the ride, appearing in forty-two of Rogers' movies, as well as fifty-six others with Charles Starrett, Autry, John Wayne, and others. Karl kept performing until literally the last moments of his life: He suffered an onstage heart attack during a performance in West Springfield, Massachusetts, on September 20, 1961, and died minutes later.

▷ **The Sons of the Pioneers. That's Karl Farr on the right. The excessive wear caused by his pick as he strummed near the fingerboard shows why pickguards are called pickguards.**

◁ **Sons of the Pioneers guitarist Karl Farr's Martin workhorse.**

▲ This 1939 Martin Ð-28
guitar was Farr's chief guitar for years,
though on knockabout movie sets he often
strummed a 1930s Miami guitar. (Whoever
made the Miami guitar is lost in time. It looked similar to
a Martin, but with a slightly rounded top to the headstock.)
The Ð-28's extra black pickguards are reputed to have been intended to make the instrument look more akin to Farr's new 1951 Fender. The pickguards do appear to have been
added about the time Farr got the Fender. Earlier photos of the Ð-28 show considerable pick
wear to either side of the fingerboard, and then a pair of tortoiseshell guards.

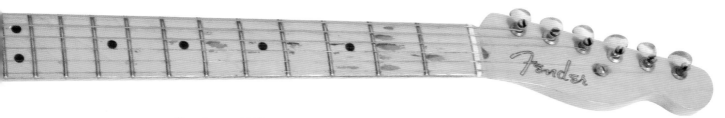

⚠ Karl Farr's 1951 Fender Broadcaster "Nocaster" guitar. This guitar was a personal gift from Leo Fender to Farr. The serial number is 0757, and it was made during a brief period in mid-1951 when no model name appeared on the headstock.

Fender's revolutionary solidbody guitar was called the Broadcaster when it was introduced in 1950. The Fred Gretsch Company, it turned out, had registered that name for one of its drum kits. Fender avoided a legal challenge by dropping the name. Until they settled on "Telecaster" and had decals made, the guitars went nameless. For decades now, collectors have referred to these as Nocasters.

⚠ Some Fender fanatics obsess over every tiny detail and variant in the instruments. This under-the-pickguard shot shows a rare feature on some early Teles: a round hole that was a mid-point for the neck pickup's wiring.

▲ Roy Rogers' fringed, lightly rhine-stoned Nudie shirt. Over his long career, cowboy star Rogers owned dozens of Nudie outfits. A good horseman who had spent much of his youth on a farm, Rogers had little use for plain old denim, preferring Nudie's garb. Along with his time on movie screens, he entertained in person, and a Nudie suit helped to give fans their money's worth. Rogers once explained, "When we rode into the arena, we looked like glittering flags, which made it easy for the kids in the back row of the balcony to see the show."

This shirt resides in the remarkable C. F. Martin Museum in Nazareth, Pennsylvania.

▲ Roy Rogers took a big chance when he quit the Sons of the Pioneers to try to become a movie star, but he never would have been on a lunchbox if he hadn't. This 1958 Thermos brand lunchbox is one of the nearly countless expressions of the popularity that Rogers and wife Dale Evans achieved.

▷ Another of Rogers'
Nudie shirts residing
at the C. F. Martin
Museum.

6

RHINESTONES AND TWANGING TONES

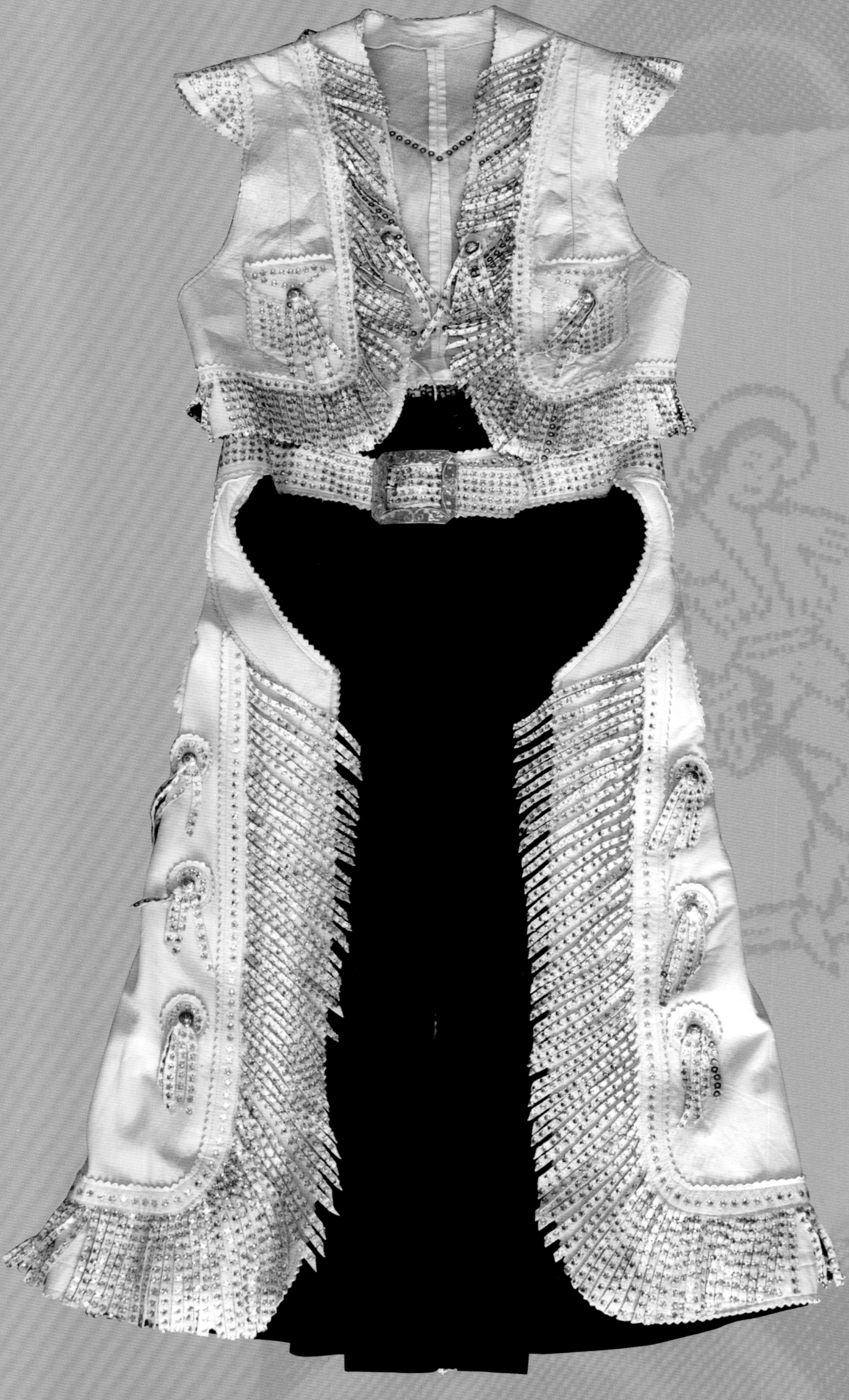

◁ **Dale Evans' 1950s** fringed Nudie outfit. Compared to the quantity of suits that Nudie decorated men with, he made relatively few outfits for women. Movie and TV star Dale Evans (along with Las Vegas country performer Judy Lynn) almost made up for that lack, faithfully buying Nudie outfits year after year. As Roy Rogers' wife and constant co-star, she had to Nudie-up or be outshone by Rogers.

Many female country singers preferred a less westernized look, and there also weren't all that many female country singers to begin with. For the entirety of the 1950s, there were only six No. 1 country hits sung by women, and three of those were duets with men. There were some gigantic female talents, but country music was largely a man's business, because the majority of country record buyers were women, and they bought records by male stars.

Chapter 2

Ken MacKenzie

In the Depression years, nearly everyone loved singing cowboys. To people living through seemingly unsolvable hard times, it was a relief to spend a few cents to see movies that hearkened to an imaginary time when there was no problem that couldn't be solved with a horse and a guitar.

Some of Hollywood's singing cowboys toured the country, but there were also regional performers like Ken MacKenzie who were never on a movie screen.

Born to Canadian immigrants in Concord, New Hampshire, in 1918, MacKenzie got his start singing on local radio when he was eighteen. He relocated to Maine, where he organized a traveling tent show that worked the Northeastern United States and Canada for thirty-five years.

Like the movies' singing cowboys, MacKenzie dressed in fanciful western garb. And like Gene Autry, he played a Martin D-45 guitar with his name inlaid on the fingerboard. MacKenzie must have done pretty well for himself: In the late 1930s, a D-45 sold for $250, nearly half the price of a new Ford coupe.

▲ MacKenzie, solo and with his troupe in the 1940s.

◀ Singing cowboy Ken MacKenzie's Martin D-45S guitar. The S stands for "Special Order," which in this case meant having his name inlaid on the fingerboard.

◁ Ken MacKenzie's 1939 Martin D-45S. By the time C. F. Martin & Co. entered its "golden age" in the 1930s, it was already the oldest musical instrument manufacturer in the United States. Born in 1796 in Saxony, now part of Germany, Christian Frederick Martin immigrated to the US in 1833, settled in Nazareth, Pennsylvania, seven years later, and set about making guitars that were a blend of old world craftsmanship and American-born invention.

The Martin guitars of the 1800s—which few real cowboys likely played—were small-bodied "parlor" instruments by today's standards. Movie cowboys preferred the larger, louder Dreadnoughts that Martin introduced in 1931. In 1933, Martin took a special order from Gene Autry to make a fancy, upscale model with abalone "mother-of-pearl" inlay and other deluxe features. That prompted Martin to issue a production version of the instrument, the D-45. They built only ninety-one of the pricy ($250) instruments before production was halted during World War II.

Chapter 3

Red Foley

Kentuckian Clyde "Red" Foley began performing in 1930 on the Chicago radio giant WLS, a station with a 50,000-watt signal that could be heard in thirty-eight states. Foley seemed just as interested in reaching a wide audience. He dialed back the twang on most of his material, and was an early proponent of describing the music as "country" instead of "hillbilly." He sang "Candy Kisses," "Old Shep," and the WWII morale-booster "Smoke on the Water" (No, not *that* "Smoke on the Water") with a croon that would have been just as at home on the pop chart, which is where Foley's songs often landed.

He wasn't a Nudie sort of guy, typically wearing a conventional suit and tie. Unlike most country singers of his era, he often didn't bother playing the guitar in performances. He certainly had some nice ones, though, including this Martin OM-18.

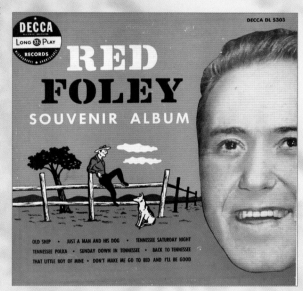

▲ **Red Foley on record.**

◬ Red Foley's Martin ΘM-18 guitar from 1930, the year the short-lived model was introduced. ΘM stood for Θrchestra Model, and it was briefly the biggest guitar C. F. Martin & Co.
made. It also had a longer neck than previous models, to make it more appealing to banjo
players, as banjos at the time were more popular than guitars. That's probably also why this
guitar has banjo tuners. By late 1931, the model came equipped with standard guitar tuners.
The elbow rest and fancy fingerboard inlays are not original. In 1934, with minor changes,
the ΘMs were given today's more familiar 000 designation.

⚠ Red Foley's tooled leather golf club bag.
Country stars liked tooled leather so much
it's a wonder none of them were buried in it.

Chapter 4

Jimmy Wakely

Singer Jimmy Wakely actually grew up in a log cabin in Arkansas, but it was on Hollywood soundstages that he found fame. He joined Gene Autry's *Melody Ranch* radio show in 1940, and subsequently starred as a singing cowboy in a series of B-movies. Some considered him—with his Bing Crosby–influenced style—to be the finest of the singing cowboys. In the years following World War II, Wakely was also one of the most successful pop and country singers in the nation. His hits included "One Has My Name (The Other Has My Heart)," "Mona Lisa," and "The Gods Were Angry with Me." Wakely's band was a training ground for a generation of California country artists, including Spade Cooley, Cliffie Stone, and Merle Haggard.

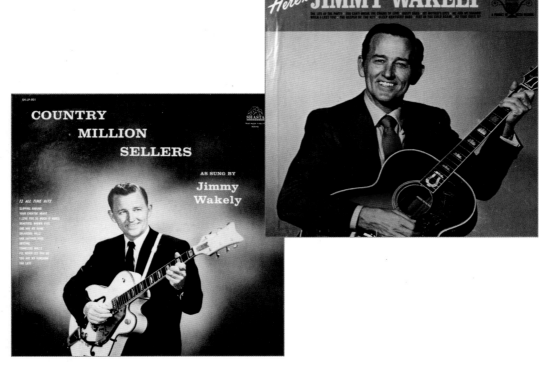

⚠ Jimmy Wakely with one of his Gretsches, and with his earlier Gibson SJ-200.

SHASTA
TRUE HIGH FIDELITY
SOUND

Y
LLION
SELLERS

GRETSCH

THE
WHITE
FALCON

31496

◁ In his singing cowboy days, Jimmy
Wakely sported a Gibson SJ-200. By the
time he was topping the pop charts, he
had switched to the Cadillac Eldorado of
hollowbody electric guitars: the Gretsch
White Falcon, with its white lacquer finish
(which fades to ivory over time), gold hard-
ware and golden "swizzle stick" binding.

Wakely owned at least two of the instruments,
and neither is quite normal. The one shown on
the album cover features pre-1958 appointments, such as the hump-block fret markers and
single pickup switch, but it sports the humbucking Filter'Tron pickups introduced in 1958.

The one in Mac's collection has a 1959 serial
number and other expected features of that era, such
as Filter'Trons, a zero fret, "thumbprint" fret markers, and a second switch, but it has a Melita bridge
instead of that year's equally clunky "Space Con-
trol" bridge. The strangest feature is the headstock:
Unlike other White Falcons, it has the black faceplate
and shape of most other Gretsch models, not the white-faced,
elongated V-shaped headstock of a White Falcon.

Chapter 5

Jimmie Dolan

Jimmie Dolan billed himself as "America's Cowboy Troubadour," and his late 1940s press biography claimed, "No singer of Western songs is better acquainted with large areas of its mountains and plains, its streams and deserts."

That was probably some publicist's whimsy, unless the South Pacific counts as a stream, since Dolan spent five years as a Navy radioman there during World War II, where he built up a fan base by singing for the troops. Before that, the Missourian was generally planted in St. Louis doing a radio show, and after the war settled in Los Angeles, where he was a regular at such dancehalls as LA's 97th Street Corral and Anaheim's Harmony Park Ballroom.

Signed to Modern Records and then Capitol, he had several well-received records, and one No. 6 country hit, 1951's "Hot Rod Race," a recited precursor to "Hot Rod Lincoln."

According to his bio, "He says his most treasured possession is his old Martin guitar." Others might agree: His 1942 Martin here was one of the last of the fabled D-45s to be made. Though referred to as "pre-war D-45s," the original run of Martin's top guitar lasted a ways into 1942, when the war effort and a scarcity of foreign woods halted production.

◁ Mac scored Jimmie Dolan's gray Turk suit and his boots for free from West Coast megadealer Norm Harris. They were thrown in with the deal for the Martin D-45, in which Harris probably made enough to keep him in suits and boots for a good while.

Nathan Turk predated Nudie as a Los Angeles western clothier. Though some of his designs bordered on the florid, he just as often produced relatively reserved suits such as Dolan's.

JIMMIE DOLAN

◁ Jimmie Dolan's **1942 Martin D-45**. It's a fine example of Martin's top of the line guitar, with its looming Dreadnought shape, delicate mother of pearl borders, and Brazilian rosewood back and sides.

Wishing you many happy hours of enjoyment from the songs I have written and included for you in the following pages — And for the pleasure of coming into your homes in this folio — Thanks a Million Times.

Jimmie Dolan

△ Jimmy Dolan.

◁ Hank Snow's
"Snow Job"
Martin Ð-45,
with pink
Nudie suit.

Chapter 6

Hank Snow

When Mac Yasuda first saw Hank Snow staring back at him from a seven-inch record sleeve, there was no hint in that face of the life Snow had lived. The ache in his voice was another matter.

Born in 1914, Snow grew up dirt poor in Nova Scotia, with holes in his shoes and bread and molasses for dinner when he was lucky. His childhood sorrows were compounded by a stepfather so cruel that, to escape him, Snow took to the sea on a fishing vessel when he was twelve. He toiled and froze on sail-rigged ships for four years, until being hammered in a hurricane that drowned six other ships and took 132 lives made firm ground seem like a better idea. There, he shoveled coal, hauled salt, sold bootleg liquor, slept on a straw mat, and survived a burst appendix in a charity hospital.

Poverty didn't vanish when he started performing. At one show in Halifax, his outfit was such a sorry sight that the theater manager made him exchange clothes with an usher before he could go onstage. In his autobiography Snow recounted, "I made a promise to myself that day—that whenever I would appear in public to sing, I would wear the most decorative outfits I could find. Throughout my life, I've kept that promise."

Once Snow found fame, Nudie certainly helped him keep that promise. After some success in Canada,

Snow came to Nashville and built one of the most remarkable careers in country music. His first US chart-topper, "I'm Movin' On," stayed at No. 1 on the country charts for a record twenty-nine weeks in 1950. Snow continued to top the charts for nearly a quarter century, and spent a total of forty-nine years on RCA records, the longest span of any artist on any label.

After meeting Mac in Japan in 1967, the two occasionally corresponded. Mac visited Snow at his home on his first trip to Nashville in 1971, and on future trips there. Eventually their star-and-fan relationship grew into friendship, though Mac remained in awe of him, even after Snow hosted him on the *Opry*. When Snow passed away in 1999, Mac was one of the pallbearers at the funeral.

◁ **Snow with Nudie Cohn.**

⚠ Hank Snow's **1950**s pink Nudie suit. Heavily rhinestoned lapels were a signature of his apparel. As Snow explained in his autobiography, "It's always been my belief that the audience wants to see, and deserves, a little flash by the artist on stage, rather than see him looking like the neighbor next door."

Snow also wore suits by Nathan Turk and, later, Harvey Krantz, but most of his closet was filled with Nudie's elaborate creations.

⚠ Snow's fawn Nudie suit with pink laurels, and buttons shaped like pearl-handled derringers, year unknown.

◁ Snow's Rainbow Ranch Boys
bandmember suit, 1950s. When
country stars outfitted their bands
with Nudie suits, the designs were
typically plainer than the star's. This
outfit was worn by Rainbow Ranch
Boy Kayton Roberts. Roberts played
guitar with Snow until switching to
pedal steel in the late 1960s.

⚠ Snow's dark blue
Nudie shirt with leather
fringe and embroidered
guitars, year unknown.

△ Snow's tan Nudie suit with pink laurels and buttons
shaped like pearl-handled derringers, year unknown.

Snow's light blue Nudie shirt with leather fringe, 1954.

HANK SNOW

◁ What better way for grown men to spend their time than by staging recreations of Hank Snow album covers? This one reassembles the items featured on one of the two covers used for Snow's *Souvenirs* album. The boots are not the pair in the original photo, though they were Snow's. The hat is just a hat, and that's not the real autumn in the background. The Martin OM-45 and the tooled leather guitar case are the real deal.

◁ Many country singers could only strum their guitars. Snow was an accomplished and distinctive soloist. One of the proudest moments in his early career was when he could afford his first Martin guitar, and he remained a Martin loyalist. The 1930 OM-45 model here was one of Snow's most prized possessions. The intricately inlaid abalone is a prime example of Martin's understated glitz.

38

RHINESTONES AND TWANGING TONES

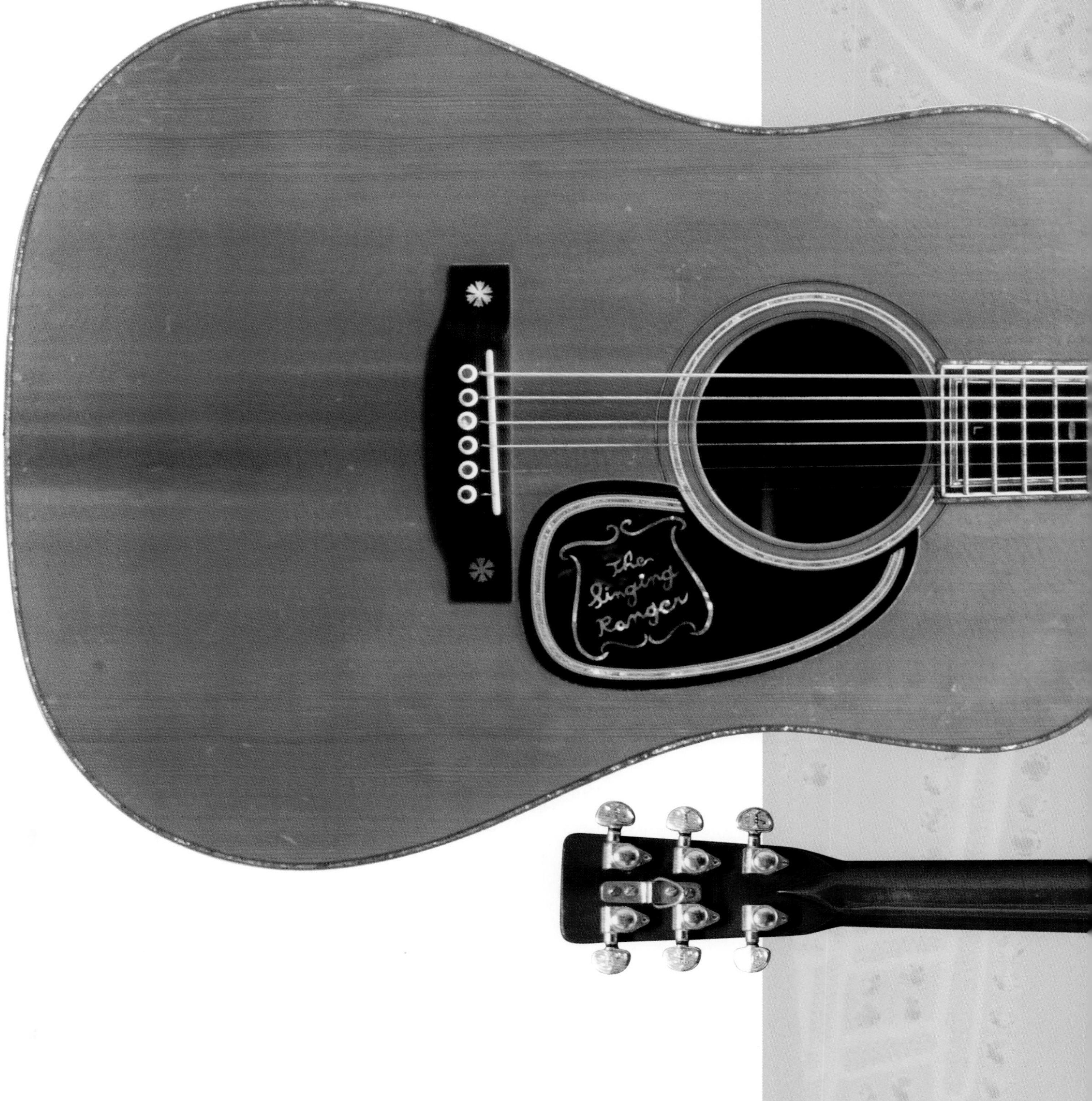

HANK SNOW

▽ Martin's booming Dreadnought guitars—which country players popularized—initially lacked the fancy inlays available on the company's daintier models, until Gene Autry special-ordered the first D-45 in 1933. Martin added the model to its line, and it was the company's most expensive model. Production halted during World War II, and afterwards the company didn't resume making its D-45 and other labor-intensive inlaid models.

Martin received requests for D-45s through the years. When one came from Snow in 1966, they listened. The company sent a new D-28 to Tennessee luthier and inlay artist Mike Longworth, who did the inlay work on his kitchen table. (Longworth subsequently went to work for Martin in Nazareth, Pennsylvania.)

Players nicknamed Snow's guitar "the Snow Job." It helped renew interest in the D-45, prompting Martin to reissue the model in 1968.

Mac recalls Snow being so protective of this guitar that every time he came off stage, he'd go directly to his dressing room and latch the guitar in its case before he'd even greet anybody.

◁ Snow with his Ð-45, at Knott's Berry Farm
in the late 1960s, and on an album cover.

Hank Snow Enterprises

P. O. Box 1084

NASHVILLE, TENNESSEE 37202

8 May 1970

R.C.A. Victor Records

WSM Grand Ole Opry & T V

Mr. Makoto Yasuda
1-banchi Koshien Harukaze-cho
Nishinomiya
JAPAN

My dear friend Makoto:

Your letter of January 12th received, and I am indeed very sorry to be this late in answering you, but I am usually away behind with my correspondence to my many friends across the world. It is indeed a pleasure hearing from you and to know everything is going along fine, and I am also very pleased to know that you received my Christmas Album and that you liked it.

In regards to the guitar I play, yes, you are correct in your thinking. I have many different types of Martin Guitars, but the D-28 is the guitar I always use, and as a matter of fact, I just - in the last three years - had a new Martin Guitar made, which was made from a D-28 and turned into a D-45. This was made especially for me, at the Martin Factory, and is a very beautiful instrument.

I also just recently purchased one of the new D-41's which is a tremendous guitar, and I believe I like the tone of this D-41 better than any Martin Guitar I have.

The D-45, that I mentioned on the D-28 which was converted to a D-45, after the inlay and the gold work, etc., or the gold plating was done, this guitar cost me approximately $1500.00. The guitar I just bought, the D-41, in the United States costs around $800.00.

In regards to Jimmy Tokita, I did not know until receiving your letter that Jimmy was back in Tokyo, or as you say in your letter, you seen him in Osaka. I had seen him on a couple different occassions while he was here in the United States, a couple of times in the state of Pennsylvania and a couple of times here in the City of Nashville. However, to my knowledge, I do not know of him ever doing a spot on the Grand Ole Opry, especially with me. I have, in other words, never seen him perform on the Grand Ole Opry.

In regards to changing members in my band, I have changed Mr. Kayton Roberts from rhythm guitar to the steel guitar which he does extremely well on, and I have changed Jimmie Widener from the bass to rhythm guitar which he handles extremely well. I have a new boy playing bass for me by the name of Bobby Wright.

Ask Your RCA Victor Dealer For My Single Records and Albums

▲ **A 1971 letter Mac received from Snow, discussing his D-45 and other guitars.**

◁ Hank Snow's early **1960**'s one-of-a-kind Gibson. It is considerably narrower than the J-200 model it is based upon, and has a deeper body, checkered trim, and other unique appointments.

⬬ Mac with the **1934** Martin Đ-28 that Hank Snow played when he first saw him in Japan, poolside at Snow's Rainbow Ranch home.

◁ Snow's custom-order Gibson.

◭ Hank Snow's Martin Ð-41, the guitar discussed in Snow's letter to Mac. This photo and the following ones of Snow's guitars and Nudie suits were shot at Snow's Rainbow Ranch home in 1999.

▷ Snow's personal Yasuda guitar, and the grape-filled Nudie suit he's seen wearing in the photo at Knott's Berry Farm.

▷ Snow's early 1930s Regal Model 27 resonator guitar, made in Chicago under license from California's Dobro Corp.

▲ Snow's "guitar" shirt, with his Martin 000-18 guitar.

▲ Snow's black floral Nudie suit and his OM-45 Martin.

◄ Hank Snow's Mossman guitar, with a Nudie suit reflecting Snow's years at sea in his youth.

⚠ A custom guitar of Snow's
from an unknown maker.

⚠ Snow's Brazilian Del Vecchio resonator guitar,
an instrument also favored by Chet Atkins.

The Singing Ranger

⌃ A custom guitar Mac had made
for Snow by Crafters of Tennessee.

▲ Snow and Mac, backstage at the Opry.

RHINESTONES AND TWANGING TONES

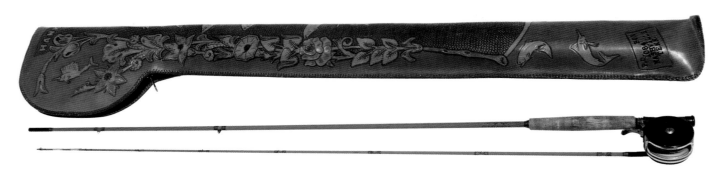

⚠ Snow's tooled leather guitar case,
briefcase, and fishing rod case.

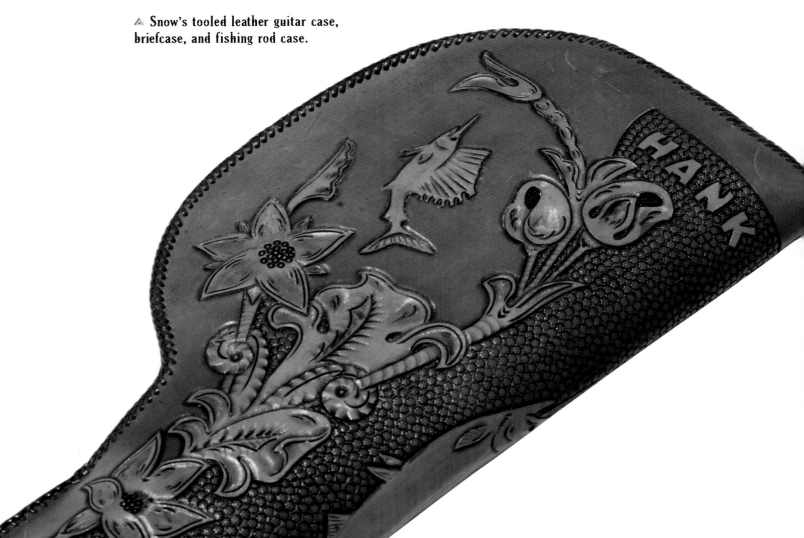

⊿ Hank Snow and
Mac, playing in
Snow's home office.

▷ The custom guitar
strap that Snow used
with his D-45.

⬧ Mac and other pallbearers at Hank Snow's funeral.

◁ For all the years that Mac visited Hank Snow at his home, the two usually met in Snow's office. Mac was never in the adjoining den until Jimmy Snow invited him to the house after Hank's funeral. There, on a wall only a few feet from where Mac had sat with Snow all those years, he was touched to find that Snow had saved and displayed the assemblage of 1,000 origami cranes that Mac and his bandmates had made for him thirty-two years before.

Chapter 7

The Willis Brothers

The Willis Brothers—James "Guy" Willis, Charles "Skeeter" Willis, and John "Vic" Willis—liked to clown around, but they were some serious talents. They started performing as a group in 1932—originally calling themselves the Oklahoma Wranglers—and continued in one form or another for over six decades, until 1995, when the last Willis, Vic, died.

The brothers grew up singing and playing music together on the family farm in Oklahoma. They were primarily a vocal group, harmonizing and trading off lead vocals. The instrumentation was fairly novel for a country group: Skeeter on fiddle, Vic on accordion, and Guy on guitar. In 1946, they were the first musicians to record with Hank Williams. They subsequently toured with Eddy Arnold for eight years, and had a long run on the Grand Ole Opry.

Chiefly playing accompaniment, Guy preferred the sort of large-bodied archtop guitars used to drive the rhythm in big-band jazz. His main guitar through the years was a handsomely hulking 1940s Stromberg Master 300, like Freddie Green used to propel the Count Basie band. Built by Boston-based master luthier Elmer Stromberg, it is among the rarest and most coveted of archtop guitars.

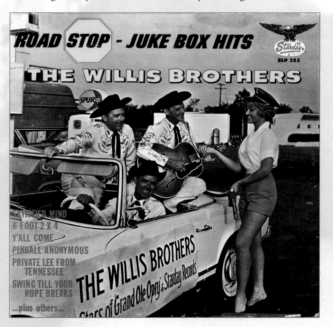

◁ **Guy Willis' Stromberg G-300, aka Master 300.**

◁ Willis' guitar was one of two models Stromberg made with a 19" lower bout, the other being the fancier Master 400. The company's serial numbers only went to around 636, and they apparently started at 300, meaning that there were only 336 archtops made between the 1930s and 1955, when Elmer Stromberg died. This one dates to the 1940s.

Chapter 8

Hank Thompson

Some talented Texans such as Jim Reeves headed east to Nashville to find fame. Others like Hank Thompson headed west. To some degree, that defined who they became. In Nashville, there was a tendency to either embrace the hillbilly side of the music, or, later, to embrace the citified and manicured Nashville Sound.

Out west, things were more unsettled and free. People wanted to dance, and country bands responded with hard-driving honky-tonk music or the big-band and Gypsy jazz–influenced western swing pioneered by Bob Wills and his Texas Playboys.

Thompson's address was in Texas (and later Oklahoma), but he practically lived on the road, averaging 260 shows a year, mostly in the western US. When not touring, he spent a lot of time in Hollywood, recording one hit after another. He sold over sixty million records in his lifetime, and had hits in six consecutive decades, which he once quipped was much easier than having them in nonconsecutive decades.

Thompson was born in Waco, Texas in 1926, and grew up listening to records by Jimmie Rodgers and Carson J. Robison, and seeing Gene Autry sing on the movie screen. Once he started putting bands together,

▲ Hank Thompson on record. His favored guitars were typically prominent on his record jackets.

◀ Hank Thompson's Gibson SJ-200 and Nudie suit.

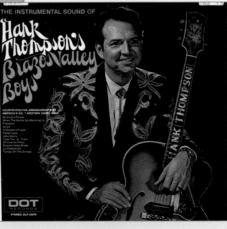

▷ Hank Thompson's 1948 Gibson SJ-200. For some players, Gibson's SJ-200 was the pinnacle of acoustic guitar design. For Thompson it was a starting point. Around 1950, he took the guitar to Paul Bigsby's small shop in Downey, California, to have Bigsby put a custom neck on it, as well as a second pickguard with Thompson's name on it. (Bigsby had already done a similar re-necking for Merle Travis, for whom he also built one of the first solidbody electric guitars.) Because the guitar's body was still a Gibson, Bigsby moved the inlaid Gibson name onto the new headstock along with his own.

The Gibson Company was not nearly so respectful when Thompson sent the guitar to its factory in Kalamazoo, Michigan for some repair work. It came back with a new Gibson neck attached, with the Bigsby neck wrapped in paper in the box. By his own account, Thompson was so furious that, "if I had been in Kalamazoo, I would have put a bomb under the place." When he had the Bigsby neck reinstalled, he also had the guitar refinished blond.

he was inspired by Wills' Texas Playboys. Unlike Wills' outfit, which prided itself on high-flying solos, Thompson retained the drive and lilt, but kept the music in the service of the vocals and the song.

That applied to his playing as well. Using a thumb pick and fingers, he could rip out a hot solo with the best of them, but spent most of his time playing rhythm and fills behind his vocals.

One can't argue with results like Thompson's 1952 "The Wild Side of Life," which was virtually the template for honky-tonk songs, and spent fifteen weeks at No. 1.

Mac first met Thompson after a college show in California in the early 1980s, where, Mac says, "He sounded just as good as his records. I was so excited I was almost crying. He was a great entertainer, and a really good guitar player." Years later, the two shared the bill on an *Opry* county fair tour.

Merle Travis and Hank Thompson, two of Capitol Record's top recording artists, had a good time together recently when Merle appeared as a guest on Hank's weekly TV show on WKY-TV in Oklahoma City.

◁ Hank Thompson's mid-1950s Gibson Super 400 CES. The Super 400 was another top-of-the-line Gibson, its finest archtop of the era. That evidently wasn't enough for Thompson, who added a gold Bigsby vibrato tailpiece with a crazy long arm, and custom inlay on the headstock, as well as his name inlaid on the fingerboard and other small customizations. He had the guitar refinished. At some point, the neck was damaged and he had Gibson replace the neck with an even more ornate one, while replacing the plastic covers on the guitar's two P-90 pickups with gold-plated ones. Throughout all these changes, it remained Thompson's main guitar for five decades.

HANK THOM

⏶ The earlier neck from the Super 400.

⏶ Thompson in his Texas home with his customized SJ-200.

▲ Thompson with his Super 400.

◁ Hank Thompson's pink Nudie suit. Mac was able to buy the two Thompson guitars at a Christie's auction in 2009, but missed out on the Thompson suits that were on the block. "They put the suits up for auction first, and I figured that if I didn't get a guitar, I wasn't going to want the suit, so I didn't bid. Then, I wound up winning both guitars; the auctions went nowhere near as high as I'd expected. Then I kicked myself for not getting a suit." The kicking stopped when he later located this jaunty number.

Chapter 9

Webb Pierce

Let's blame this guitar on Adolf Hitler, shall we? Prior to World War II, any country singer with $250 could buy a Martin D-45 with eye-catching mother of pearl ringing the body and inlaid in the fingerboard. Once the war started, prowling German U-boats made Brazilian rosewood and other imported tonewoods hard to get. Martin's inlay craftsmen were off in a foxhole somewhere. And since few musicians had $250 anyway, once the war was over Martin didn't resume making D-45s.

So when the great honky-tonk singer Webb Pierce wanted a fancy guitar, he evidently entrusted some glue-fumed goober with a trowel to customize his 1946 herringbone D-28.

The perfidy of this guitar knows no bounds: The veritable sidewalk of abalone circling the body; the clunky block letters on the neck; the name repeated in mailbox letters on the headstock, in case you missed it on the fingerboard.

Pierce deserved better. A fine singer and entertainer, he had a thirty-year run of ninety-seven hits, landing fifty-five of them in the Top Ten. Those included the barroom classic "There Stands a Glass," and his No. I hit version of Jimmie Rodgers' "I'm in the Jailhouse Now." To celebrate that song's success, a suit Nudie made for Pierce featured prison bars. Another was covered in glistening spider webs, Nudie's play on Pierce's first name.

Mac doesn't remember how he wound up with this guitar. Can you blame him?

◁ **Webb Pierce's 1946 Martin D-28, customized by an unknown party.**

including:

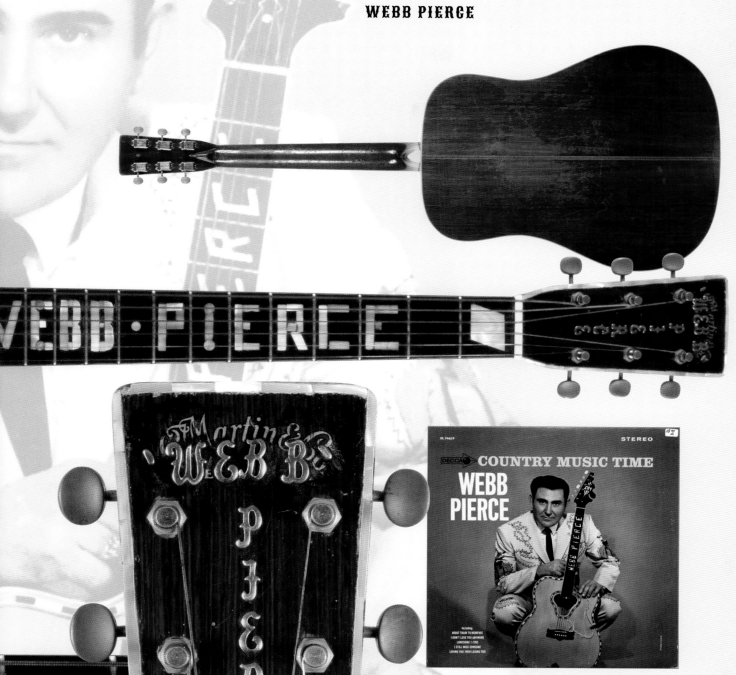

▲ When Pierce replaced his Ð-28, he got a guitar that defied anyone to make it gaudier than it already was: a crazy, fancy mess of a Frank Gay guitar.

Chapter 10

Hank Williams Haywire Hayride Guitar?

Though he never saw his thirtieth birthday, in his short lifetime Hank Williams became one of the most influential and revered songwriters and singers in country music. Williams' natural craftsmanship and open emotion in "Move it on Over," "Mansion on the Hill," "I'm So Lonesome I Could Cry," "Cold, Cold Heart," "Hey, Good Lookin'," "Jambalaya (On the Bayou)," and dozens of other songs proved that artistry and popularity were not necessarily sundered qualities.

Williams learned to play guitar from an African-American bluesman named Rufus Payne on the streets of Williams' hometown of Mount Olive, Alabama.

A charismatic performer, when Williams first appeared on the Grand Ole Opry on June 11, 1949, the audience went so wild over his rendition of "Lovesick Blues" that they called him back for six encores of the song.

Interviewed by music critic Ralph J. Gleason in 1952, Williams described his songs as "Folk music. Folk music is sincere. There ain't nothin' phony about it. When a folk singer sings a sad song, he's sad. He means it."

Williams didn't mind adding some showbiz glitz to his authenticity. He was one of Nudie's earliest customers, and often performed in a striking white suit with black musical notes embroidered on it. In 1951, Williams and his wife opened Hank and Audrey's Corral, Nashville's first store to feature the California-made clothing of Nudie and Nathan Turk. When he died, he was buried in one of his Nudie suits.

Williams' performances grew spottier over the years, as alcoholism, pills, and constant pain from a back injury wore away at him. In August of 1952, he was fired from the Opry for his no-shows and drunkenness. Williams spent that New Year's Eve being driven to a distant show in a baby blue Cadillac he'd recently purchased. It was only the next morning that the driver realized he'd been hauling a dead man around.

Williams died just as his song "I'll Never Get Out of this World Alive" was climbing the charts.

◁ **A 1941 Martin D-28, possibly owned by Hank Williams.**

▷ During his brief career, Hank Williams owned several guitars, most of them Martin Dreadnoughts. The D-28 here dates to 1941, made just before Martin's production slowed to a crawl during the Second World War.

It may or may not have been Williams' guitar. There is no documentation to prove it so. Mac bought it from Mark Taylor, who got it from Bill Monroe's guitar player Joe Stewart, who claimed it had been Williams' guitar, and that the repair visible on one side was the result of a collision with the Louisiana Hayride's stage one night when Williams was a mite wobbly. At the very least, the D-28 had belonged to Joe Stewart, one of the finest rhythm guitar players in bluegrass.

HANK WILLIAMS HAYWIRE HAYRIDE GUITAR?

⚠ The scene of the crime.

Chapter II

Porter Wagoner

In his long and successful career, Porter Wagoner was both an icon and iconoclast. He was bona fide country, from his farmboy roots to his stunning Nudie suits. He earned fans' loyalty with his heartfelt songs, professionalism, and a work ethic devoted to always giving his audiences the best shows he could.

Wagoner also tested his fans' loyalty by following his muse where it took him. Before Nashville had quite adjusted to drums being allowed on the Grand Ole Opry, Wagoner was experimenting with disco beats. After being bowled over by a James Brown performance, he famously hosted Brown on the Opry, an event that some Opry regulars refused to attend. Before the notion of "concept albums" became a rock staple, Wagoner was recording ones themed on alcoholism, insanity, and the homicidal side of life. Songs such as his "Rubber Room" featured some of the wildest production and sound effects ever heard in country music.

Wagoner was born in 1927 on a farm near West Plains, Missouri. He earned the $7 for his first guitar by trapping and skinning rabbits. He'd sing standing on a tree stump pretending it was the Opry stage, prompting a neighbor boy to tell him, "You're as close to the Grand Ole Opry as you'll ever get. You'll be looking at these mules in the rear end when you're sixty-five."

Even that prospect seemed beyond reach when the family farm was sold to pay debts in 1943. Wagoner found work at a shoe factory, then a butcher shop, where the owner liked his voice and sponsored radio spots for the young singer. His broadcasts garnered thousands of fan letters, and he was signed the following year, 1952, to RCA Records. By 1954 he was a regular on the Ozark Jubilee TV show and had his first hit, "Company's Comin'," followed in 1955 by the smash "A Satisfied Mind." In 1957 he became a member of the Opry, with nary a mule's hind regions in sight.

Nudie sought him out early in his career and made a suit for free. Wagoner subsequently bought and wore over fifty Nudie suits.

Wagoner's records caught Mac's ear in Japan, both because he heard the emotion in his songs, and because he heard those songs at all. Wagoner's label, RCA, was nearly the only one that bothered promoting country artists in Japan.

Mac eventually became good friends with Wagoner, having shared the Opry stage and tours with him. The two spent a lot of time together at Wagoner's home and Opry dressing room. Most of the Wagoner suits and guitars Mac has came directly from him, or semi-directly.

◀ **Porter Wagoner's tools of the trade.**

▲ **A 1960s Japanese Wagoner 45, showing his Martin D-28.**

"The first guitar I got that meant a lot to me was Porter's Gibson J-200. He originally wasn't interested in selling his stuff, but long before then he had given one of his two J-200s to Norma Jean (Wagoner's duet partner until she was replaced by Dolly Parton). So I went to her house and asked if she'd be interested in selling it, and she said, 'Sure, I can't stand that guitar.'

"'Why?'

"'Because it was Porter's.' She still didn't like that he'd replaced her with Dolly Parton."

Onstage and off, Wagoner and Mac were prone to engaging in good-natured ribbing. The day Mac got the J-200, he took it to Wagoner's Opry dressing room to show him, announcing, "Hey, Porter, look what I got."

"You brought my old guitar from my home?"

"No. This one's mine now! But you can sign it."

Wagoner was sufficiently bemused by Mac's gumption that he relented and sold Mac his other Gibson and several suits.

▲ Wagoner's J-200, given to his singer Norma Jean.

⚠ Wagoner early in his career, with the J-200.

⚠ Norma Jean beside Wagoner, with the J-200.

PORTER WAGONER

▽ Wagoner's Gibson SJ-200N. Though a Martin Đ-28 was Wagoner's workhorse guitar for much of his career, his main instruments in his earlier days were a pair of Gibsons: an SJ-200N and a J-200N. (The chief difference in the models was the name, which changed in the early 1950s, along with minor cosmetic differences. The "N" in both cases signifies a natural blond finish.) Along with its robust tone, the J-200's rounded shape fit with the wagon wheels on Wagoner's suits.

He told Mac he retired them from his tours—he logged 120,000 highway miles in 1956 alone—because he didn't want anything to happen to them. It was a prudent concern: His main Martin Đ-28 was stolen on a tour.

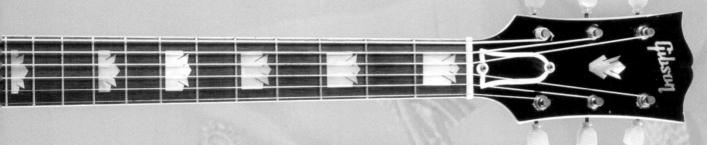

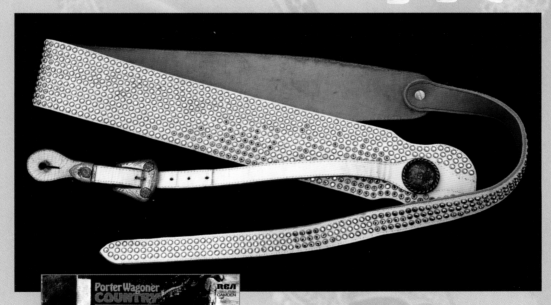

△ Wagoner's Nudie guitar strap.

◁ Wagoner on the porch with his Gibson SJ-200.

⚠ Wagoner's turquoise Nudie suit, year unknown.

Shy by nature, Wagoner compensated by wearing some of the loudest suits in the business. When he couldn't afford the $350 for a Nudie suit in the 1950s, Nudie gave him his first suit for free. (He's wearing that suit on his 1962 *A Slice of Life* album.) Recalling that first suit, Wagoner told an interviewer, "It was breathtaking! People would just go *'aaah'* when I'd come on stage at times. When the lights hit 'em, it would be really exciting."

Wagoner went on to buy over fifty Nudie suits, most with the wagon wheel motif Nudie came up with as a play on his name.

RHINESTONES AND TWANGING TONES

⚠ Wagoner's white Nudie suit, year unknown.

89

PORTER WAGONER

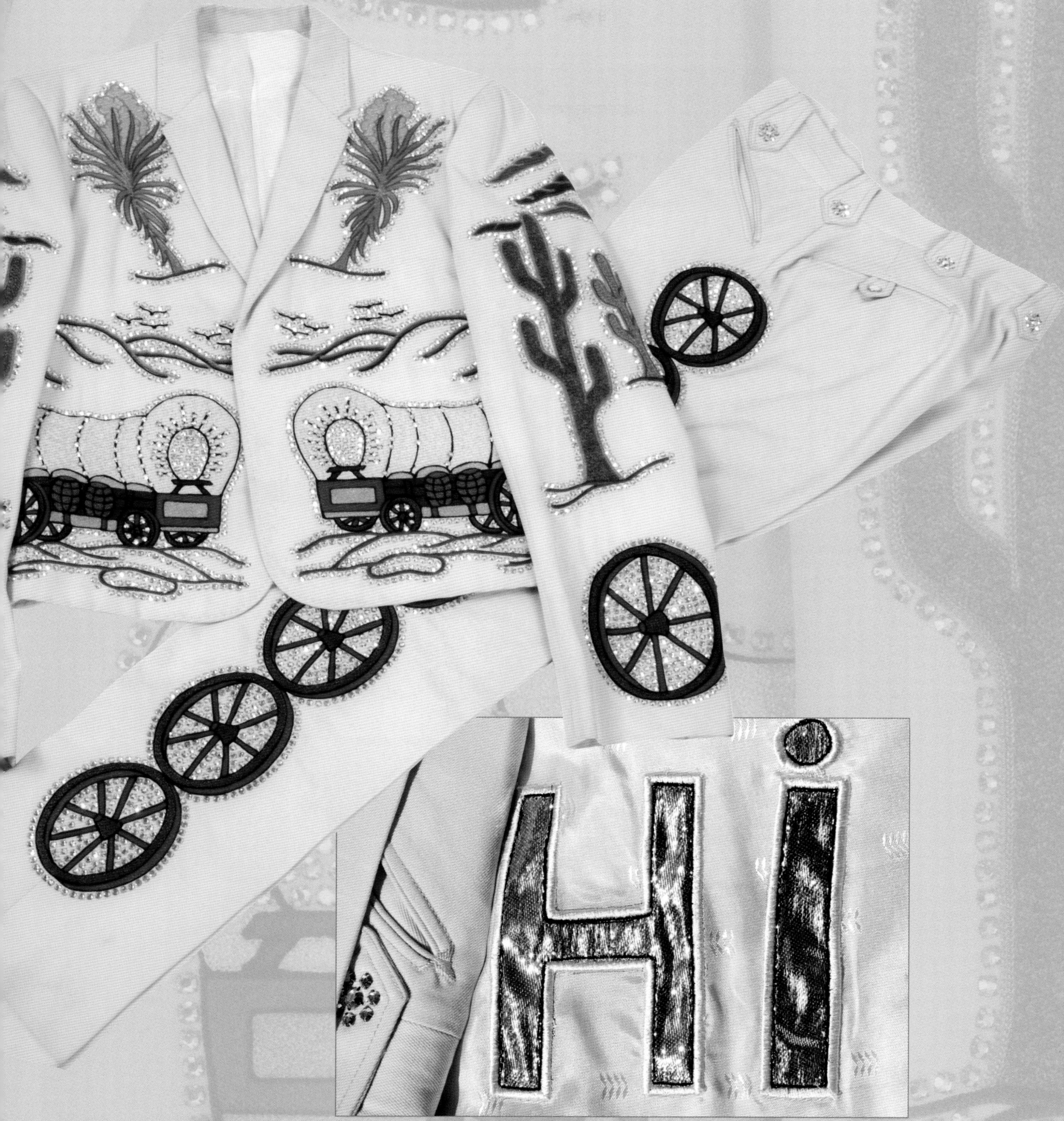

▷ Mac and Porter Wagoner cutting up on the Grand Ole Opry stage.

⚠ Wagoner's violet Nudie suit, with "Hi" embroidered in the lining, year unknown.

▲ Wagoner's black Nudie suit, 1980.

△ Wagoner's light
blue Nudie suit, 1982.

⚠ Wagoner's black floral pattern Nudie suit, year unknown.

△ Wagoner's red Nudie suit, 1957.

◁ A Carl Smith
Gay guitar and
Nudie suit, names
to reckon with.

Chapter 12

Carl Smith

Carl Smith had one of the most durable careers in country music. In 1950, the second record he made, "Let's Live a Little," went to No. 3 on the country charts, and he had hits in each of the next twenty-four years. He likely would have had more, but he retired from music near the end of the 1970s (emerging only to record one more album in 1986). Smith was busy following his other passion of raising horses. He passed away in 2010 at the age of eighty-two.

Smith was born in 1927 in Tennessee, and he was performing on local radio shows before he was out of high school. In between his thirty-one Top Ten hits in the 1950s, Smith found time to act in a few films and TV shows, and to marry singer June Carter in 1952 (they divorced four years later, and she eventually married Johnny Cash), and then singer Goldie Hill in 1957. Both wives sang with Smith, and one of Hill's Nudie outfits is seen here.

△ Early in Smith's career, he favored wild, fringed cowboy outfits. Later, perhaps realizing his movie star looks were enough, he settled upon more citified suits, like the one here, with Porter Wagoner.

⚠ Like many other country performers, he bought Nudie suits the way other people buy socks. The rainbow of Smith's suits here gives a small idea of what some stars' closets looked like.

⚠ Goldie Hill's 1950s red stage outfit, likely made by Nudie though it lacks a label. Argolda Voncile Hill was from Texas. In 1953 she scored a No. 1 record with "I Let the Stars Get in My Eyes" on the male-dominated country chart. She married Carl Smith in 1957, and probably hung up this dress then, because she largely retired from show business aside from the occasional recording session. That's pretty much how things were then.

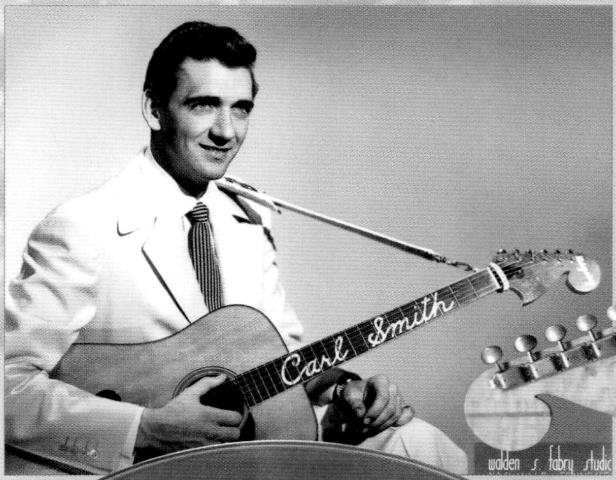
Carl Smith
walden s. fabry studio

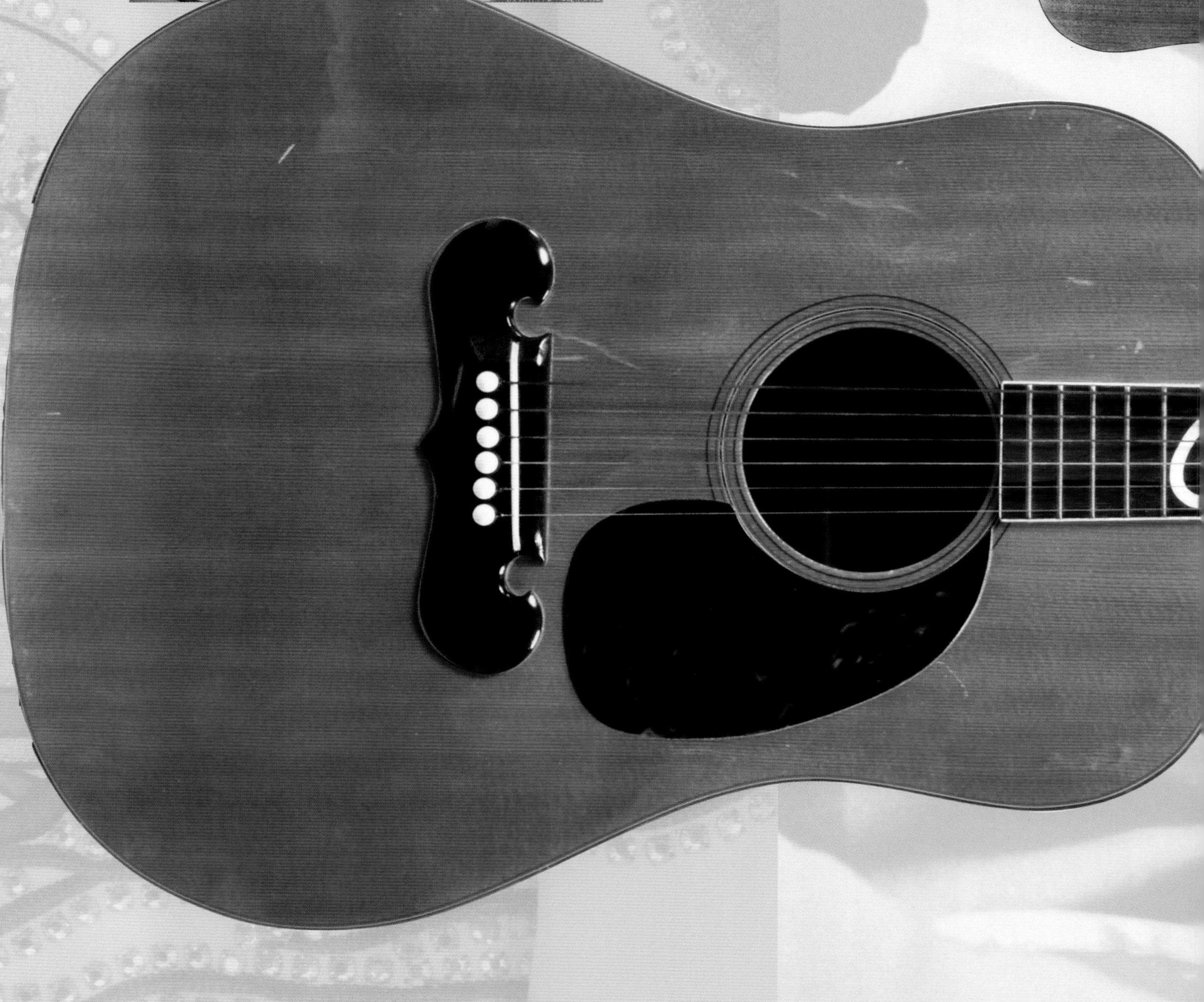

⚠ Though country artists loved Martin guitars, they also loved to monkey around with them. Not content with the austere beauty of most Martin models, performers gussied them up with gleaming inlays, fanciful bridges, and oversized pickguards. Smith had his 1946 D-18 modified by Paul Bigsby, a Southern California machinist and motorcycle buff who in the 1940s built one of the first solidbody electric guitars. Bigsby also designed a vibrato tailpiece for guitars that is still popular today. Many of the top players in the nation turned to Bigsby's little shop for their electric guitars, double-necks, steel guitars, and mandolins.

As Bigsby did for Hank Thompson and other guitarists, around 1953 he replaced Smith's D-18 neck with one of his own, with a slimmer, faster-playing profile and a headstock design that likely influenced Leo Fender's necks. And in case anyone in Smith's audiences forgot whom they'd come to see, Smith had his name inlaid on the fingerboard.

⚠ Archtop guitars were pioneered by Kalamazoo, Michigan, guitarmaker Orville Gibson, and became popular in the early 20th century because their violin-like design produced a bit more volume. C. F. Martin & Co. was a latecomer to the archtop field, and their 1930s models only had a middling success. The Depression-sapped economy assured that its top-of-the-line F-9 hardly sold at all. In its best year, 1931, only twenty-eight F-9s were sold. They were discontinued in 1942, and became rarer still in the 1960s, when guitarists began having their F-9 and F-7 Martins converted into flattops.

Smith's 1936 F-9 avoided that fate, though it did fall victim to his and other country players' penchant for affixing the largest pickguards imaginable to their instruments.

◎ 105 ◎
CARL SMITH

▷ A set list taped to Smith's F-9.

HEY JOE
THERE SHE GOES
I OVERLOOKEDAN ORCHID
I LOVE YOU BECAUSE
SHE CALLED ME BABY
DEEP WATER
LET OLD MOTHER NATURE
IF TEARDROPS WERE PENNIES
I NEED HELP
MAMA BEAR
FOGGY RIVER
BEST YEARS OF YOUR LIFE
ARE YOU TEASING ME
MR MOON
THERE STANDS THE GLASS
LOOSE TALK
DON'T JUST STAND THERE
WABASH CANNON BALL
DREAMING AGAIN
BACK UP BUDDY
YOU WIN AGAIN
F..ED LOVE AND WINTER ROSES
TIME CHANGES EVERYTHING
GOOD DEAL LUCILLE

"SMITH'S THE NAME"

CARL SMITH

CARL SMITH

◁ Rather than modify a Martin, why not get a guitar that's garish to begin with? Canadian guitarmaker Frank Gay built some of the most outstandingly outlandish country guitars ever. Curiously, the Edmonton-based luthier mostly built classical guitars, and only a handful of the flashy star guitars he's remembered for now. Smith's 1950s one is a standout example, with a crenulated peghead, chunky inlaid binding, and butterfly pickguards, again bearing Smith's name. (The Gay name on the peghead was replaced when it was repaired in Nashville's Sho-Bud pedal steel guitar factory.)

△ In the early 1960s, the Fender company—which had revolutionized electric guitars and basses—opted to begin manufacturing acoustic guitars designed by German builder Roger Rossmeisl, who had previously created some of Rickenbacker's most distinctive instruments. Unlike most acoustics, the Fenders had a bolt-on neck, and a metal tube inside the body to take stress off the top.

Leo Fender was a fan of country music, and made sure its star players were well equipped with his instruments. Smith's Palomino, with a rare black finish, likely dates to 1968. It and Fender's other acoustics were discontinued the following year due to lack of interest.

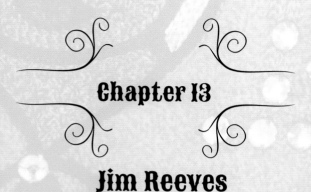

Chapter 13

Jim Reeves

Jim Reeves grew up poor in rural Panola County, Texas, one of nine children of a widowed mother who worked in the fields to support them. Though he was a sharp student, Reeves quit college to work in a shipyard during World War II. Also an athlete, he was signed to the St. Louis Cardinals until an ankle injury closed that door. He instead became a truck driver, boxer, insurance salesman, and radio announcer.

While announcing for Shreveport's *Louisiana Hayride* in 1952, Reeves got his break, inadvertently thanks to Hank Williams. The troubled legend went AWOL one night, and Reeves was asked to fill in. A record label rep heard him sing and signed him on the spot. Reeves' first record the following year, "Mexican Joe," became a No. 1 country hit.

His earliest music had a hillbilly twang, but Reeves developed a smoother style that helped define and popularize the urbane "Nashville Sound." Reeves' gentle lilt, applied to songs like "He'll Have to Go" and "I Love You Because," resulted in huge international crossover hits. That latter song was the longest-charting record of 1964 in England, during the height of Beatlemania. Reeves was even popular in Africa, where decades later, Nigerian *Juju* music sensation King Sunny Adé cited Reeves as one of his biggest influences.

Tragically, at the height of his popularity, on July 21, 1964, Reeves crashed his airplane in rough weather in the dense woods outside of Nashville. He was so beloved that posthumous releases of his recordings continued to top the charts years after he was gone.

Mac became a fan when he first heard Reeves on a compilation album in Japan, and was excited decades later when he found his concert promoter friend Ed Gregory had bought many items from the Reeves museum when it closed. Gregory was a Tennessee businessman who ran carnivals at county fairs and other venues, and who promoted the Grand Ole Opry tours in which Mac performed.

Gregory's memorabilia from several country performers was stored haphazardly in a Nashville warehouse. Mac found the Martin D-28 that had been Reeves' companion on the Grand Ole Opry and hundreds of other stages, "was just laying on a shelf collecting dust, not even in a case."

He bought that and Reeve's rarely-seen Martin 000-45 from Gregory, and regrets not also buying Reeves' one-of-a-kind blue Rickenbacker there.

◁ **Jim Reeves' Martin 000-45 and Nudie suit.**

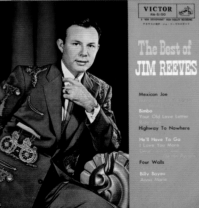

▲ Jim Reeves owned several Nudie suits, but in keeping with his "Gentleman Jim" nickname, he typically performed in a tuxedo (usually purchased at Nashville's Cain-Sloan department store). Ed Gregory's trove had none of Reeves' Nudie suits. Mac eventually found and purchased two elsewhere, but was bothered that he couldn't find any photo of Reeves wearing the blue suit. Walking past a small record shop in Japan one day, he had a premonition, and in their "folk music" bin found a reissue LP with the suit on the cover.

The jacket has faded due to sun exposure from the years it was displayed in the Jim Reeves Museum in Nashville.

⚠ Two other photos have since surfaced of Reeves wearing the blue suit, taken at a 1950s University of Houston show by western swing mandolinist Scotty Broyles. That's Broyles' wife with Reeves in the offstage photo.

◄ This second Nudie suit that Jim Reeves owned had a Native American theme, a more peaceful, domestic one than was typical for the era.

⚠ Reeves' 1940 Martin 000-45. Like a great many acoustic country players, Reeves favored Martin guitars. The 000-45 model was once the flagship of Martin's line, both its largest and most ornate guitar, featuring a subdued yet stunning mother of pearl inlay. By the time Reeves got his in the 1950s, such pre-war Martins were already coveted instruments. Reeves said that he wrote several songs with this guitar.

JIM REEVES

⚠ In 1931 Martin introduced guitars that overshadowed the 000's "grand concert" size: its Dreadnought line, named for the largest class of battleship. Most of the advances in guitars have been in response to players' pleas for louder guitars that wouldn't be drowned out by other band instruments. The sound of Martin's Dreadnoughts have been likened to cannon fire by players, one reason why they became hugely popular with country musicians. Reeves' 1957 D-28 here is as fancy as the line got in that decade. During the privations of World War II, Martin discontinued its inlaid models.

Chapter 14

Hank Locklin

When Lawrence Hankins Locklin was nine, he was hit by a school bus. Just like that, his young life was knocked off-course and into a painful, often lonely convalescence at his family's Florida farmhouse. He decided to learn the guitar. If he had regrets, he put them into song, and went about his life as an enduring and affable fellow.

He started performing on a Pensacola, Florida, radio station in his mid-teens. Emboldened by his local success, Locklin quit high school and toured the honky-tonks and radio studios of the South. He started recording in the late 1940s, and sold more than fifteen million records over his long career. 1960's "Please Help Me I'm Falling" spent nine months on the country chart, with fourteen weeks at No. 1, helping to popularize the new citified "Nashville Sound." "Send Me the Pillow that You Dream On," which he wrote in 1949, has been covered by everyone from Roy Rogers to Dean Martin to Van Morrison.

Locklin's good-natured demeanor and plaintive voice made him a natural goodwill ambassador, and he helped spread country music to audiences in Europe, Japan, and other distant climes. Nudie's suit designs often played up aspects of the wearer's background or career, and Locklin's international status was the source for the two of his famous suits shown here.

Mac became a fan when he was still a teenager in Japan, and for decades he wanted the singer's Gibson SJ-200 guitar. When the two became friends on the Opry shows, Mac would periodically bug Locklin about the guitar and his retired Nudie suits, with Locklin always insisting he could never sell the guitar.

One day Mac got a call. Locklin had cancer, needed money, and the guitar was for sale. Mac was glad to give him an exorbitant sum for the guitar and two suits, and then was surprised when Locklin told him, "One thing: Don't tell anybody I sold this guitar to you."

"Why?"

"Well, it's not my guitar."

"What do you mean? It's on your album

◁ **Hank Lockin's Gibson SJ-200N and "Irish" suit.**

⬈ **Hank Locklin with his guitar, and a relatively sedate suit.**

covers! You've always had that guitar!"

"No, in the fifties, Carl Smith loaned it to me, and I never returned it."

Mac did some searching, and discovered an early 1950s photo where Smith was indeed posing with the same guitar. Mac already owned a number of Smith's guitars and stage outfits, and contacted Smith about the SJ-200. He found that Locklin had been worried about nothing for decades: Smith had always considered the guitar a gift.

⚠ Hank Locklin's Nudie "international" suit, from the late 1950s. The global landmarks arrayed on Locklin's Nudie suit here can refer equally to his international success and to the around-the-world theme of his 1958 album *Foreign Love*, which boasted such songs as "Geisha Girl," "Fraulein," and "Mademoiselle."

△ Hank Locklin's Nudie "Irish" suit, circa 1963. Locklin was proud of his Scots-Irish heritage, and he was hugely popular in Ireland. He let them know the feeling was mutual with his 1963 concept album *Irish Songs Country Style*. It was only natural that he and Nudie would come up with an Ireland-themed suit.

▲ Locklin's Gibson SJ-200N. Second only
to Martin guitars, country singers chose Gibsons to be their traveling companions. Nearly
as often, they chose the company's J-200 model
(originally dubbed SJ-200 until the early 1950s). The
broad, rounded looks of the J-200 bore no relation to small-bodied guitars
made in the old cowboy days, but it had just the look for a cowboy star sitting around the
campfire under a Technicolor sky. Country performers found they looked great on an auditorium
stage as well.

Originally known for its archtopped guitars, Kalamazoo, Michigan-based Gibson began
horning in on Martin's flattop territory in 1926, and in 1937 made its first SJ-200 for
singing cowboy Ray Whitley. Hank Locklin's 1951 natural-finished SJ-200N (it was more
commonly available in a shaded sunburst finish) came factory-equipped with a "mustache"
bridge, large imitation tortoise shell pickguard with etched floral pattern, and a fingerboard
with crown-shaped inlays.

▷ Locklin and Mac backstage on one of the Opry 1990s tours.

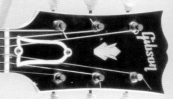

SHE'S BETTER THAN MOST

"THE TUNE SMITHS"
JOHNY - SAMMY - CARL - VELMA - HAL

▲ An early photo of Carl Smith with Locklin's SJ-200.

Chapter 15

Billy Walker

Born in the West Texas town of Ralls in 1929, Billy Walker saw a Gene Autry movie at age thirteen and determined that a singing cowboy's life was better than anything in his immediate environs. He earned money for his first guitar by plucking chickens, and at fifteen entered and won a talent contest, taking home $3, a chocolate cake, and a spot on a Clovis, New Mexico, radio station, to which he'd hitchhike eighty miles. After graduating from high school, Walker formed a trio and toured around Texas, wearing a mask, as "the Traveling Texan, the Masked Singer of Country Songs."

He didn't stay masked for long, and by 1952 Walker was a regular on the Louisiana Hayride radio broadcast out of Shreveport. His recording career took off two years later with the Top Ten hit "Thank You for Calling." He became a member of the Grand Ole Opry in 1960. Through that decade and the 1970s, Walker had a run of hits, with "Charlie's Shoes," "Willie the Weeper," "Cross the Brazos at Waco," "Ramona," and "She Goes Walking Through My Mind" being but a few.

Along with being an engaging and dynamic entertainer, Walker had a reputation as one of the nicest guys in country music. He and Mac met at the *Opry* in the early 1990s and became fast friends, golfing and traveling around Japan together. In March, 2006, Walker performed at the opening of the *Rhinestones and Twangin' Tones* exhibit at the Fullerton Museum Center in Southern California.

Sadly, that was one of his final performances. Walker died two months later when his tour van crashed on Interstate 65 in Alabama, bringing a close to his nearly six decades devoted to country music.

"I went to his funeral, but I couldn't stay," Mac recalls. "There were just too many memories for me."

◁ Billy Walker's
Martin D-28.

⚠ Walker early in his career,
with Nudie suits that perhaps
went up in marital flames.

⚠ Billy Walker's white suit with Native American patterns is the
work of Harvey Krantz, a Southern California clothing designer
who specializes in western wear. This suit is a good example of
his understated (relative to Nudie) style.

"Billy had some Nudie suits, but he told me his ex-wife burned
them up when they divorced," Mac says.

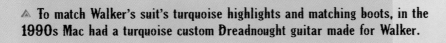

⚠ To match Walker's suit's turquoise highlights and matching boots, in the 1990s Mac had a turquoise custom Dreadnought guitar made for Walker.

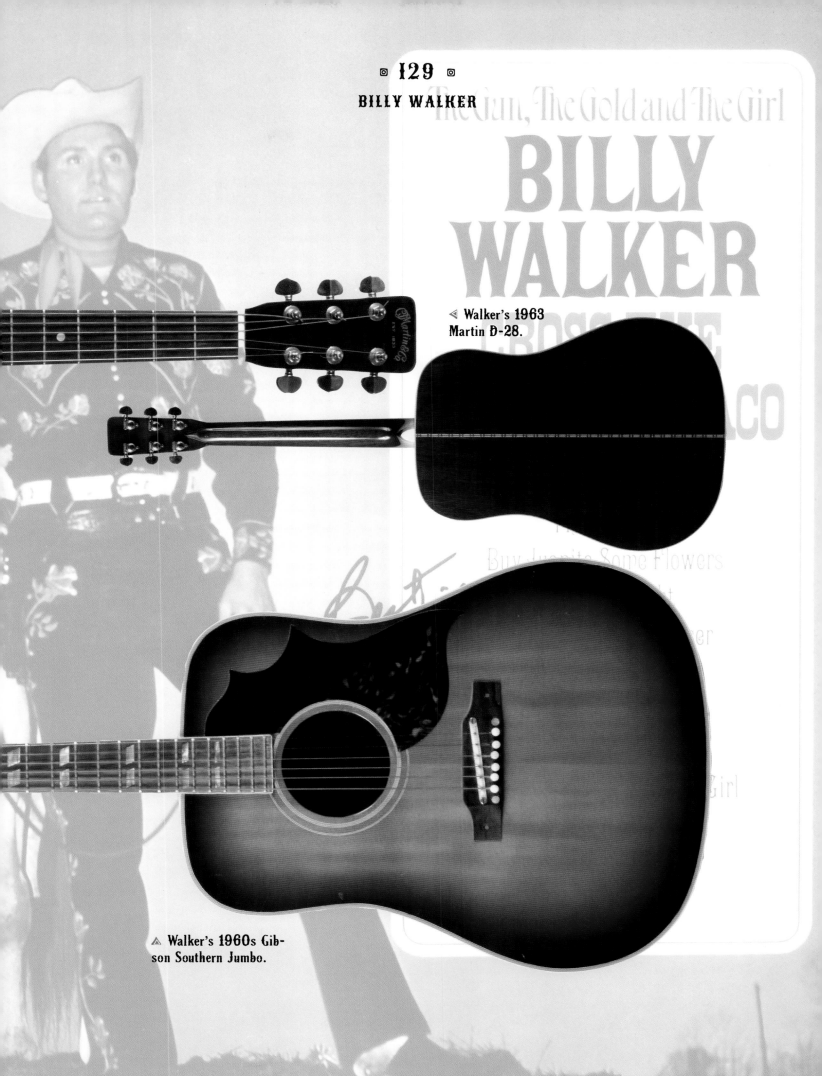

◄ Walker's 1963
Martin D-28.

▲ Walker's 1960s Gib-
son Southern Jumbo.

Chapter 16

Jack Greene

Tennessee-born Jack "Jolly Greene Giant" Greene was in several fancifully named outfits, including Clyde Grugg and the Tennessee Valley Boys, the Cherokee Trio, the Rhythm Ranch Boys, and the Peachtree Cowboys, before joining Ernest Tubb's Texas Troubadours in 1962 as a drummer.

Tubb encouraged Greene to step out as a vocalist, and featured him both in his own band and as an opening act. In 1965, Tubb pushed him out of the nest, with the understanding that Greene would be welcome back if his solo career didn't work out.

That wasn't necessary. In 1966 his "There Goes My Everything" went to the No. 1 slot for seven weeks and his career went on from there. Though the hits stopped coming in the 1970s, Greene kept going, touring and recording until 2010.

Greene was a close friend of Billy Walker, who was close friends with Mac, so the three spent a lot of time together. Mac helped organize a Japanese tour for Greene, while Greene and Walker both sang backup on Mac's album. Even after Greene was suffering from Alzheimer's, he remained a strong performer, remembering the words to his songs after he had forgotten many other things, Mac says.

Mac bought the guitars from Greene. He had hoped to also get some of his Nudie outfits, but learned that a wife of Greene's had discarded them decades before.

⚠ **Greene on record.**

◁ **Jack Greene's Gibson Super 400.**

△ For a drummer, Greene strummed a pretty choice guitar: The Gibson Super 400 model was the longtime pinnacle of Gibson's archtop guitar crafts-manship. While other Gibson guitars were often produced in the thousands, this Super 400 is one of only forty-four that the company built in 1948. Greene bought it to replace another Super 400 that had been stolen early in his career.

◁ Later in his career, Greene performed with this 1970s Gibson L-5 guitar.

⬟ Greene onstage at the Opry.

Chapter 17

Ferlin Husky

Along with having one of the most country-sounding names in all of music, Ferlin Husky also owned one of its most glaringly countrified guitars. With its unique body shape, shield-shaped sound hole, florid bridge design, and an inferno of inlay, it would be the rarest, most enigmatic Gibson guitar extant, if it were a Gibson.

Despite the name on the headstock, it was actually built in the 1950s by Frank Gay, the Edmonton, Canada, luthier who built distinctly strange guitars for several country artists. The Gibson factory later did repairs on the neck joint, and added their name to the guitar.

It's the sort of instrument that could easily overshadow a performer, but not Husky. The Missouri-born singer was practically a hayseed Danny Kaye onstage, skipping, making faces, singing his heart out, imitating other entertainers, and rolling out his "comic philosopher" alter ego Simon Crum at the drop of a hat. Husky also acted, mostly bit parts in films, though he strode fearlessly into the lead role in *Hillbillys in a Haunted House*, a film much more ghastly than even its title suggests.

Husky's long singing career first took off in Southern California in the early 1950s. His hits on Capitol Records ranged from antic rockabilly like "Bob Cat Bop" to a maudlin recitation about dead children on the highway in "The Drunken Driver." His more mainstream hits included "On the Wings of a Dove," "A Dear John Letter," and "Gone."

▲ **Husky by the fire on an early LP.**

◁ **Ferlin Husky's Gibson-branded Frank Gay guitar.**

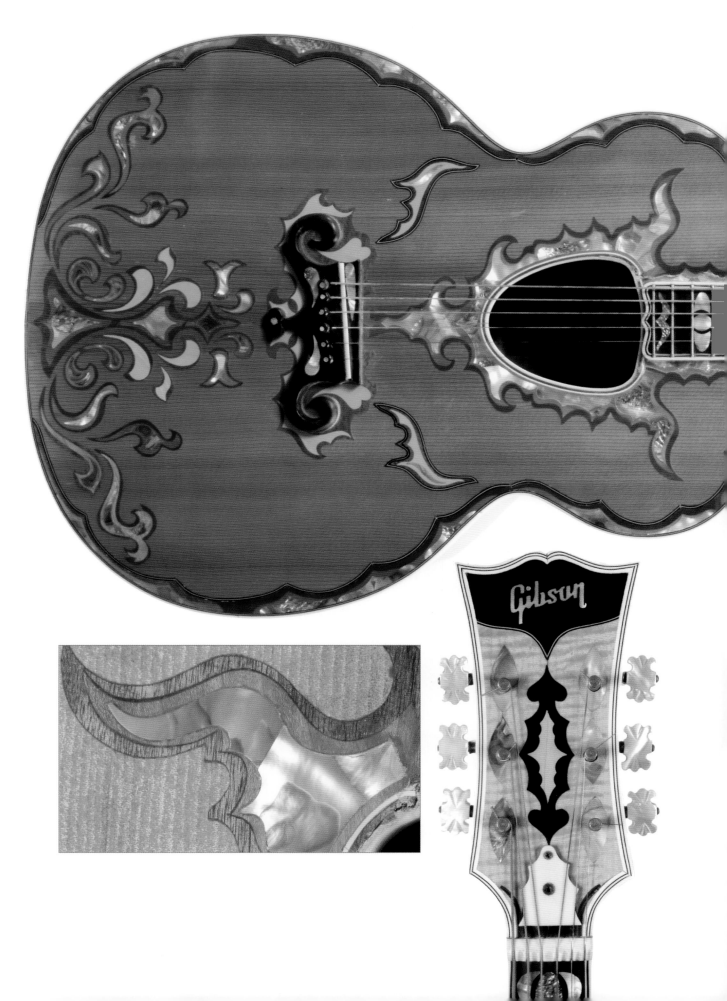

FERLIN HUSKY

◁ In the 1950s, no one was making stranger acoustic guitars than Edmonton, Alberta's Frank Gay.

△ Husky, in the hay with his Gay guitar in the film *Country Music on Broadway*.

Chapter 18

Jimmy C. Newman

It can't have been easy for Nudie coming up with design ideas once he started clothing rock stars: How do you attire "the introspective one" of a group, or decide which rhinestone pattern best represents an LSD trip?

Country presented few such quandaries. A star has an Irish name? Shamrocks and dudeen clay pipes for him. A man in black? Got it covered.

And Nudie had just the thing for an Alligator Man.

Country music has numerous tributaries, and Jimmy C. Newman came down a bayou byway. Born Jimmy Yeve Newman near Big Mamou, Louisiana, he grew up playing Cajun music, which had its roots in French fiddle reels, filtered through Canada and a wealth of hardship before arriving in the swamplands of Louisiana. For Cajun's influence on country, one needs look no further than Hank Williams' "Jambalaya."

Newman's career spanned the mid-1940s to 2014 (when he still appeared on the *Grand Ole Opry* up until two weeks before he died). Many of his thirty-three hit records were straight-ahead country, and some were considerably bigger than his 1966 "Alligator Man," but that song hung on him like a suit.

So that's the suit Nudie made, bedecked with gators in a rainbow of rhinestone-bordered colors. When Newman wore one suit out, he'd buy another like it.

Mac knew Newman well, and bought his suit and Martin D-18 guitar directly from him. For the remainder of his career, Newman played a custom guitar Mac made for him, with gators on it, of course.

◁ **A Martin guitar with a goofy pickguard: check. A loud Nudie suit: check. Jimmy C. Newman was equipped for country stardom.**

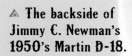

△ **The backside of Jimmy C. Newman's 1950's Martin D-18.**

⚠ Newman's **1960**s Nudie suit, in which he was literally up to his ass in alligators.

⚠ Newman with his Đ-18 and his gatored-up Yasuda guitar.

△ Faron Young's
livid pink Nudie suit.

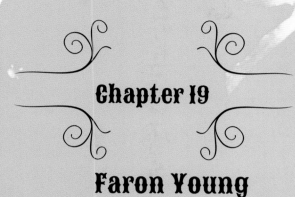

Chapter 19

Faron Young

When America first heard Faron Young on the radio in the early 1950s, the Louisianan was in Army drab instead of a Nudie suit. Just as his career on Capitol Records was taking off, Young received his draft notice; news, he later said, that made him "cry like a rat eating a red onion." He was in basic training when his "Goin' Steady" became a No. 2 hit.

Out of the service in 1955, he hit the top of the charts with songs like "Live Fast, Love Hard, Die Young," "I've Got Five Dollars and It's Saturday Night," and young songwriter Willie Nelson's "Hello Walls." Young continued to have hits well through the 1970s (his last was in 1989), this despite his tongue being practically severed in a 1971 auto accident. It required four operations to reattach, and the slight lisp in his singing after that only further endeared him to his fans.

▷ **This suit, made for Young in 1960, was not one of Nudie's wilder designs, but it's still a showstopper. It was certainly Young's best-known stage outfit.**

◁ Young also took some of his trade to Southern California clothier Harvey Krantz, who made this black shirt and pants with copper piping.

⬚ A young Faron Young.

Chapter 20

Carl Story

Though Carl Story isn't as storied a name as Bill Monroe or the Stanley Brothers, he was a seminal figure in bluegrass music. Born in Lenoir, North Carolina, in 1916, he played fiddle in Monroe's band in 1943, but before and after that he led the Rambling Mountaineers, one of the earliest Southern Appalachian bluegrass bands, distinguished by sterling musicianship and tight harmonies.

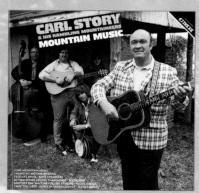

Story's keening high tenor rode herd over the proceedings, while his Martin D-28 kept things chugging along. He wasn't a showoff player; instead his bass lines and brief fills were in service of the songs. Gospel was always a large part of Story's repertoire, and it became the dominant theme of his recorded output, much of it on the Starday label.

◁ Story's Đ-28, with the requisite country appointments of a sprawling, abstract-shape pickguard and his name inlaid in the fingerboard.

▲ Carl Story's weathered Martin Đ-28.

Chapter 21

Wilma Lee Cooper

Wilma Lee Cooper was playing bluegrass music decades before that name was coined for it. Where she grew up in West Virginia it was pretty much the only music they knew, passed down through generations of family, few more so than Cooper's. She was born Wilma Lee Leary in 1921 into the musical Leary family, who were so representative of their region's music that they were recorded by the Library of Congress.

After she married band fiddler Stony Cooper in 1939, the two formed Wilma Lee and Stony Cooper and the Clinch Mountain Clan. The pair became popular performers on the WWVA Jamboree radio program, and then joined the Grand Ole Opry in 1957. After Stony's death in 1977, Wilma Lee continued as a solo performer until she suffered a stroke while performing on the Opry stage in 2001.

She was a fine guitarist—playing taut solos and driving rhythm—and used an equally fine guitar, a pre-war Martin D-45. Actually, she had three of them, and after Mac pestered her enough, she sold him the most beat-up of the three.

⬆ Wilma Lee backstage at the Opry with the D-45S, prior to a restoration by Massachusetts luthier TJ Thompson that spanned eight years.

◀ Wilma Lee's 1939 Martin D-45S, pre-restoration.

⚠ The guitar in all its glory. The correct tuners on
the headstock cost more than a decent used car.

151

WILMA LEE COOPER

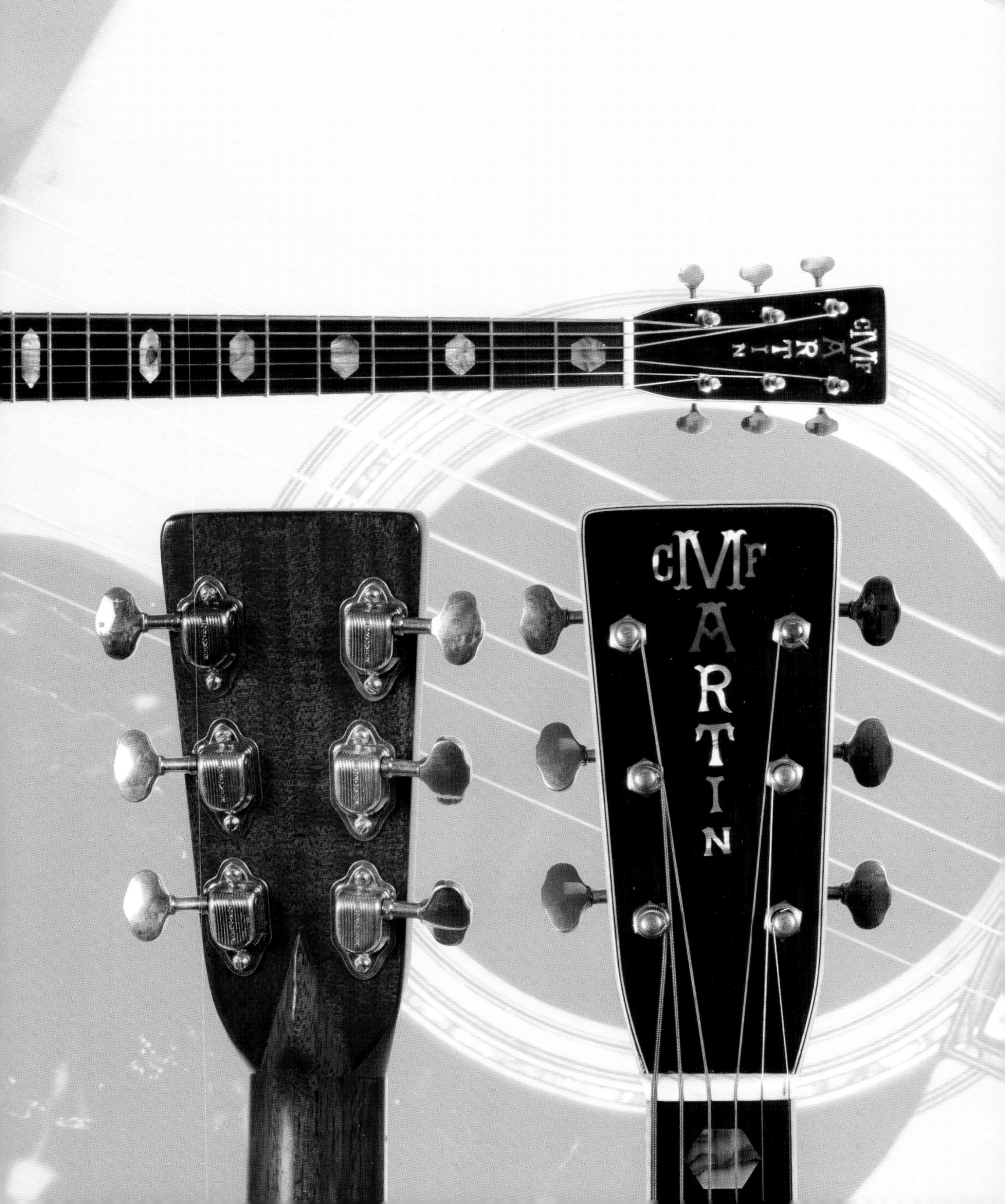

▷ Red Smiley's 1938
Martin D-45.

Chapter 22

Red Smiley

The first time Arthur "Red" Smiley saw Don Reno perform, banjoist Reno was onstage at the Grand Ole Opry with Bill Monroe, while Smiley was a diesel mechanic sitting in the audience. When they next were in the same place, it was on a more equal footing: In 1949, Smiley was playing with Virginia-based fiddler Tommy Magness' band, and suggested the bandleader hire Reno.

In 1952, Smiley and Reno made some recordings for King Records; one of which, Reno's "I'm Using My Bible for a Roadmap," became a bluegrass gospel hit. They formed their own band, the Tennessee Cut-Ups, in 1954, and for a decade Reno and Smiley were two of the most beloved and influential players in bluegrass.

Smiley was born in Asheville, North Carolina, in 1925, and played guitar semi-professionally with several Carolina- and Virginia-based outfits. He performed with Reno and the Cut-Ups until 1964, when they amicably went separate ways. Smiley mostly performed in West Virginia, where he had a TV show. Because of war injuries and diabetes, he was never in great health, and he retired briefly in 1968. By the end of the decade, he reteamed with Reno, and the two continued performing until Smiley, then only forty-six years old, died from complications of diabetes in 1972.

⚠ Smiley with Don Reno and the band.

⚠ Mac Yasuda in the 1970s, more thrilled than he looks to be playing Red Smiley's guitar, which was also the first vintage D-45 he'd handled. It was to be decades later and half a world away that he renewed his acquaintance with this guitar.

Mac had been a big fan since he was a teenager and heard Reno and Smiley on a Japanese compilation album. He was floored when, in 1976, he made one of his guitar-hunting trips to Nashville and found a special guitar waiting there.

"It was the first pre-war D-45 that I was able to play, and more than that, it was *Red Smiley*'s guitar. That's a very, very famous guitar among bluegrass players. I was so excited to see and play it!"

An associate of George Gruhn's was selling it. Even though Mac had been wheeling and dealing in guitars for years, the $8,500 price wasn't something he could afford. By the time he could, Smiley's D-45 had vanished into the mist.

It turned out that Mac's advocacy for vintage guitars in Japan hadn't just created a market for the ones he brought over; it also created competitors. Decades after Mac had played Smiley's D-45, he found that a Japanese collector had it on display in a hotel he owned called the Hotel California in the Japanese resort town of Kita Karuizawa. The owner also had another cannon of a guitar, David Bromberg's 1938 D-45, thus assuring there'd be plenty of boom at the Hotel California.

Mac eventually heard through a vintage dealer that Bromberg's D-45 was for sale, and he was able to work a deal to also buy Smiley's D-45.

After finally getting an instrument for which he'd longed for decades, did Mac feel a sense of completion?

"Sure, for a little while."

WALL AROUND YOUR HEART

SPEEDIN' (John Hardy) UNWANT

JIMMY CAUGHT THE DICKENS (Push

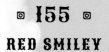

◎ 155 ◎
RED SMILEY

◁ Some players babied their top-of-the-line Martins. Not Smiley. This guitar was his constant companion for decades, and he played the hell out of it. The Brazilian rosewood back was replaced with a Đ-28's (with different center-seam marquetry and no abalone inlay) before Smiley owned it. Most of the other road wear was his doing. The bridge was replaced. "Red" was etched into the 12th fret marker, and the headstock got some extra glitz.

Chapter 23

Rem Wall

If Rem Wall was a country star, it was in a smaller firmament than the one where most stars shined. Born in Indiana, he spent his career as a regional performer in southwest Michigan. When Wall had a charting record on Columbia Records in 1963, he didn't tour to promote his career, instead staying home in Kalamazoo to care for his wife, who had multiple sclerosis.

His local career made him a star and hero to many people around Kalamazoo. In 1950, Wall began hosting *The Green Valley Jamboree* on local TV station WKZO, where he and his Green Valley Boys remained for thirty-six years. Wall was a fine performer, and touring stars made it a habit to drop in on his show.

Above all that, Wall was loved and respected for the welcome and encouragement he gave to aspiring local musicians. "He would give anyone a chance. That's just how he was," his son Ren Wall recalls.

When Rem wanted his 1947 sunburst Gibson L-5 personalized and refinished green in the early 1950s, he took it to his day job, which was at the Gibson factory. The green finish may be unique among Gibson archtops, and predates the company's general use of custom color finishes.

In his thirty-seven years at Gibson, Wall held a number of positions, and was on hand for some signature moments. When Seth Lover's humbucking pickups were first installed on a Les Paul Standard, Wall was the in-house player asked to demonstrate it for Gibson execs. He was also one of the few people on the planet to ever play a Gibson Moderne, taking one with him to a German industrial fair in 1958.

◁ **Rem Wall's distinctively green 1947 Gibson L-5 guitar, thanks to a refinish by Gibson in the 1950s. The custom pickguard from that same time crumbled and was later replaced by Gibson.**

△ **Rem Wall at the WKZO studios in the early 1950s.**

⚠ How Green was the Green Valley Boys' valley? Just about this green. A rare Gibson color.

⚠ Wall and band in the early 1960s. Wall had switched to a Gibson-made Epiphone Frontier with wild custom pickguards.

Rem's suit here is a Nudie. He had a few, but his son Ren recollects them being donated to charity.

⚠ Wall with the Green Valley Boys and their gear in the 1950s.

▷ Sonny James' 1963 prototype Epiphone Excellente. Unlike the 1964 production model, it has a smaller, plainer bridge and pickguard, more in line with the Martin guitar he played.

Chapter 24

Sonny James

Born James Loden in Hackleburg, Alabama, in 1928, Sonny James had an upbringing that was rooted in country music. Taught by his musician parents, he was nicknamed "Sonny Boy" and was singing onstage and playing mandolin by the time he was four. In his teens he appeared with the old-timey Loden Family on most of the major country radio programs, including the Louisiana Hayride and the Big W Jamboree.

After a stint in the military in Korea, James came to Nashville, where his friend Chet Atkins introduced him to Capitol Records A&R man Ken Nelson, who signed him and suggested the name change to Sonny James.

Despite his straight country background, James became one of the biggest crossover successes in country music, with twenty-one of his twenty-three hits also landing in the pop charts. His "Young Love" spent nine weeks at No. 1 in 1957, and the hits kept coming into the 1980s.

James was identified with this Epiphone Excellente guitar for much of its career. A company esteemed for its arch-top jazz guitars, Epiphone was purchased by Gibson in the late 1950s, and it became a second brand for Gibson-built

⚠ **Though James said he typically recorded with his Martin, he was quite obliging about posing with his Epiphone.**

instruments. Epiphone models were generally less lustrous than their Gibson counterparts, but the Excellente was a stellar exception, being the only Gibson-made acoustic of its era with a rosewood back and sides, and with other deluxe appointments such as "cloud" fingerboard inlays. James' Excellente was a prototype with the pickguard and other features differing from the production model.

Mac bought the guitar through George Gruhn, and recalls, "Later, Billy Walker introduced me to Sonny at an awards show. He was a good guitar player, and I asked him why he sold the Excellente, since it was always with him on his album covers and photos. He said he didn't like the Excellente much, that it didn't sound nearly as good as his Martin D-28, which was what he actually played on his records."

Mac loves the sound of the guitar. In a 1999 *Vintage Guitar* article by Walter Carter, James sounded more kindly disposed towards it himself, saying, "It was beautiful and easy to note, much easier than the Martin, and it had a sweeter sound to it." The D-28, however, had the sound people expected on his records, so he stuck with it. For that reason, he told Carter, he never officially endorsed the Excellente, but he was grateful enough for the gift that he displayed it on his records and promo shots for years. Need we mention that James' nickname was "The Southern Gentleman"?

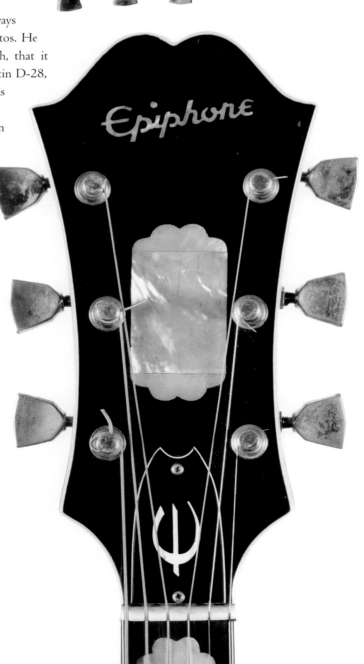

▽ **The Excellente living up to its name.**

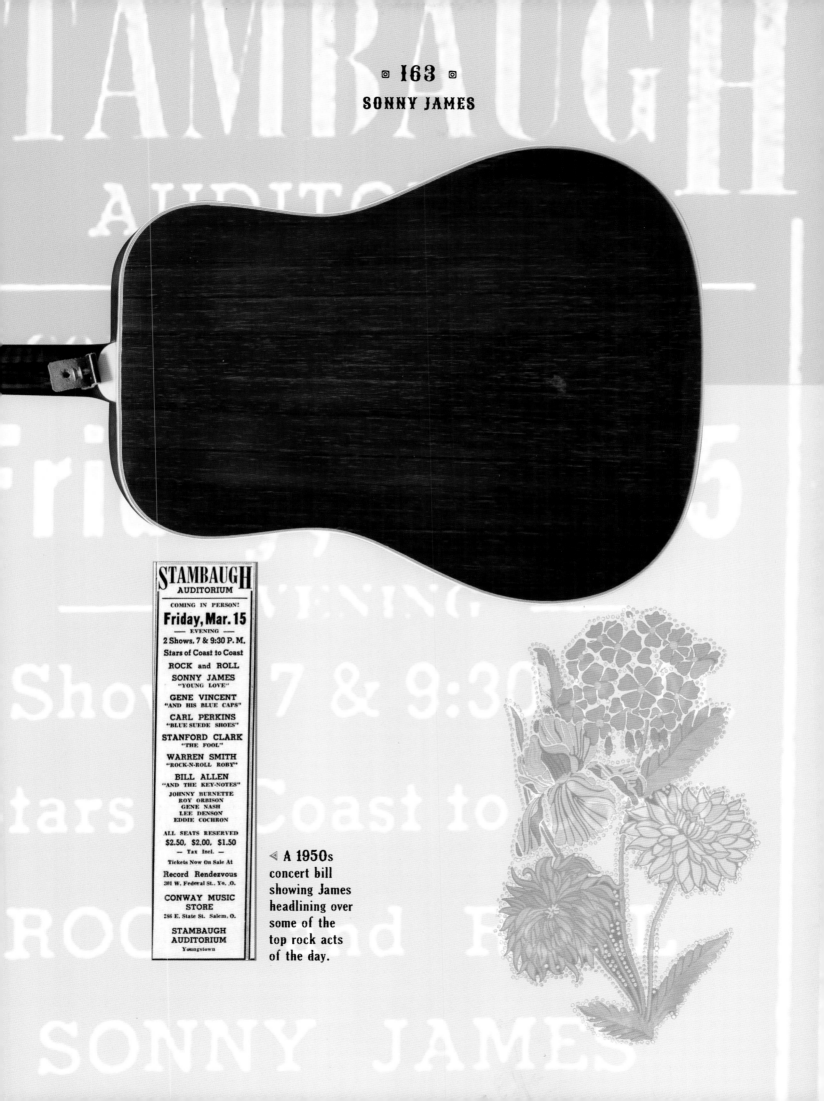

STAMBAUGH
AUDITORIUM

COMING IN PERSON!

Friday, Mar. 15
— EVENING —
2 Shows, 7 & 9:30 P. M.

Stars of Coast to Coast

ROCK and ROLL

SONNY JAMES
"YOUNG LOVE"

GENE VINCENT
"AND HIS BLUE CAPS"

CARL PERKINS
"BLUE SUEDE SHOES"

STANFORD CLARK
"THE FOOL"

WARREN SMITH
"ROCK-N-ROLL ROBY"

BILL ALLEN
"AND THE KEY-NOTES"

JOHNNY BURNETTE
ROY ORBISON
GENE NASH
LEE DENSON
EDDIE COCHRON

ALL SEATS RESERVED
$2.50, $2.00, $1.50
— Tax Incl. —
Tickets Now On Sale At

Record Rendezvous
301 W. Federal St., Yo. ,O.

CONWAY MUSIC
STORE
286 E. State St. Salem, O.

STAMBAUGH
AUDITORIUM
Youngstown

◁ A 1950s
concert bill
showing James
headlining over
some of the
top rock acts
of the day.

▷ Buck Owens' guitar strap could double as a billboard.

Chapter 25

Buck Owens

At a time when Nashville had a near stranglehold on country music, the Bakersfield sound emerged, though that sound originally had only one practitioner: Buck Owens.

Full of Fender Telecaster twang and driving rhythms, Owens' music was a raw antidote to the ever-more-produced Nashville sound of the late fifties and the sixties. He told the *LA Times*, "Out here in the western part of the United States, there weren't any Grand Ole Oprys or schoolhouse shows. Out here they had dances and honky-tonks, and if you couldn't play music they could dance to, you couldn't get a job. So I was always accustomed to a lot of beat and driving-type music."

Beginning in 1959, Owens had a run of seventy-five charting singles (with twenty No. 1s and forty-two in the Top Ten). The fun went out of it for him following the death of his guitarist and right hand man Don Rich in 1974, and six years later he retired. Dwight Yoakam urged Owens to begin performing again in 1987, and even at seventy-six years of age, he continued performing every weekend at his Crystal Palace club in Bakersfield, delivering his last performance hours before he died on March 25, 2006.

◄ **Buck Owens in Japan.**

△ Buck Owens never owned this Epiphone Excellente, but he played it on a short 1970s tour of Japan that Mac had helped facilitate (while also directing a movie of the tour). The Gibson-built, Martin D-28-inspired Excellente was a favorite of Mac's. Owens took a liking to it as well, so Mac loaned it to him for the shows.

BUCK OWENS

⚠ In the 1960s, Owens had a red, white, and blue acoustic guitar made by Bakersfield neighbor Semie Moseley of Mosrite guitars. A demand grew for such a guitar when Owens started playing his on the *Hee Haw* TV series when it debuted in 1969. He entered a licensing deal with Chicago guitarmaker Harmony to produce a copy based upon the company's Sovereign flattop. It retailed for $99 at Sears and other outlets. Owens sent this one to Mac as a thank you, along with the personalized leather strap he'd used on the Japan shows.

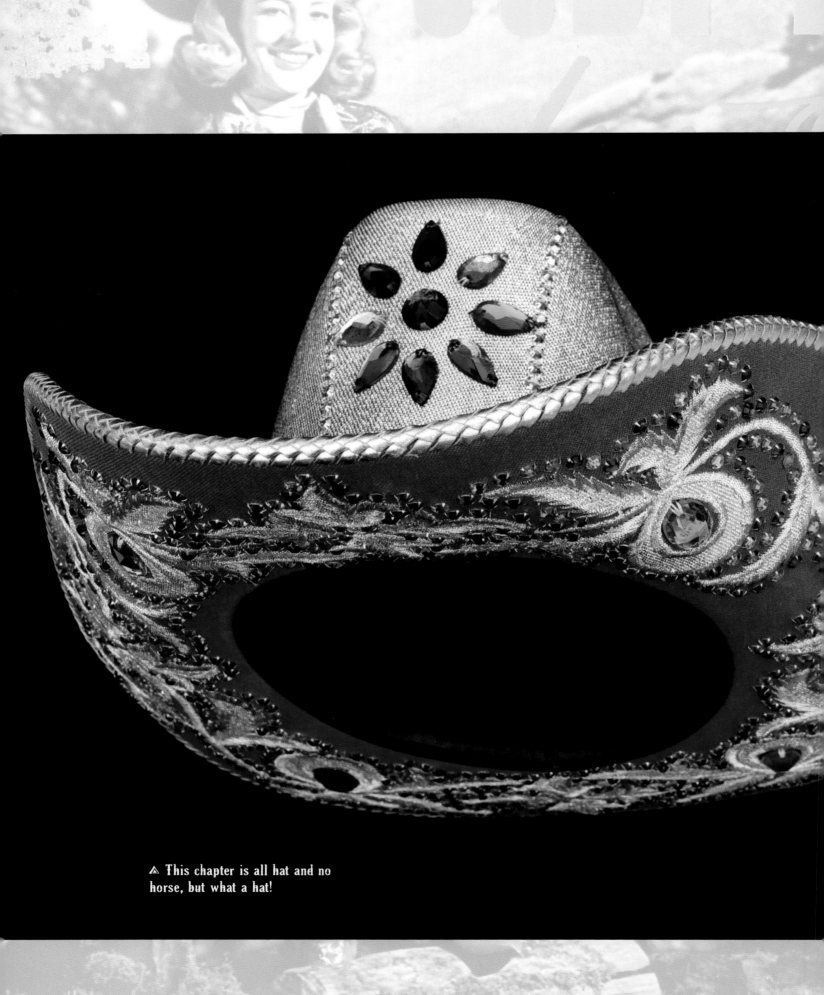

⚠ This chapter is all hat and no
horse, but what a hat!

Chapter 26

Judy Lynn

TV and movie star—and occasional singer—Dale Evans did a lot of business with Nudie, but few female country singers had many of his garments. Judy Lynn did her best to make up for that. Her seemingly endless array of Nudie's garments was an integral part of her show. Her concert programs featured photos of her clothes closet, ready to implode under the weight of her Nudies. *Music Row*, in its 2010 obituary of Lynn, described her as "the most flamboyantly costumed country star of her generation."

The daughter of bandleader Joe Voiten, she was born Judy Lynn Voiten in Boise, Idaho. She was named America's Champion Yodeler in her teens in 1953, and two years later, as Miss Idaho, was a runner-up in the Miss America pageant.

Lynn's recording career started in 1952, and continued to 1977. Only a few of her records made a dent in the charts, and she didn't rely on them for success, instead becoming a fixture in Las Vegas showrooms, first at the Golden Nugget and then at Caesar's Palace. In 1980, she quit show business to become a minister.

Perhaps that's why this hat she ordered was still sitting unsold at Nudie's Rodeo Tailors when Mac was shopping there before it shuttered in 1994.

America's Western Sweetheart. JUDY LYNN, pictured with just a portion of her fabulous $75,000 wardrobe, which was exclusively designed and tailored for her by Nudie of Hollywood.

⚠ **Performing in Las Vegas and Reno, Lynn had to compete with a lot of glitz. Nudie made sure she was well-equipped.**

▷ One of the more than fifty hats Judy Lynn ordered from Nudie.

Chapter 27

Bobby Lewis

Beautiful though it is, Bobby Lewis' Gibson SJ-200 is not the guitar he's known for. Rather, it's the guitar that drove him to the guitar that he's known for.

Born in Hodgenville, Kentucky, in 1942, Lewis began performing on the radio at age thirteen. Even with an assist from Roy Acuff, it was a decade before he had a hit record in 1966, the aptly titled "How Long Has It Been?"

By then, Lewis had already jettisoned his SJ-200. They're fine guitars, and Lewis had gone to the trouble of having his name splayed across the top. The problem was that Lewis—5' 4" tall and slender—tended to disappear behind the SJ-200's ample bouts.

He replaced it with a lute-shaped guitar. According to a 1966 article, "He didn't decide on it as a trade gimmick, but because this instrument is small and gives him a chance to be seen!" It did become a hell of a gimmick, though. The instrument is prominent on most of his album covers, while his press releases dubbed him, "The Boy with the Lute!" (Picky people will note that Lewis' wasn't a real lute, just a six-string guitar shaped like one.)

⬚ Lewis early in his career, and somewhat obscured by his Gibson.

◁ Bobby Lewis' Gibson SJ-200 guitar.

▷ Most modern players know this model as the J-200. When it first went to market in 1938, Gibson called it the Super Jumbo. The following year, they added the $200 list price to the name, to arrive at SJ-200. By the early 1950s, it was simply the J-200.

BOBBY LEWIS

▷ Lewis after he
went for the lute.

Chapter 28

Charlie Walker

Texas singer Charlie Walker had a string of classic country hits in the 1950s and 1960s, including "Pick Me Up On Your Way Down," "Close All the Honky Tonks," "Don't Squeeze My Sharmon," "The Lord Knows I'm Drinkin'," and "I Wouldn't Take Her to a Dogfight."

His 1953 Martin 000-28 was something of a consolation prize for Mac, and a reminder to him to pay more attention to people.

"Charlie Walker used to follow me around backstage at the Opry bugging me to buy a guitar from him. I was there to perform and visit with my friends, and didn't have much time for him. I'd never seen him performing with a guitar, so I figured he must not have much of anything.

"Eventually, he caught up with me, and I asked him if he had anything good to sell. He said, 'No, but I had one last year and tried to talk to you about it but didn't get a chance. I didn't think you wanted it, so I sold it to George Gruhn.'"

It turned out it was a pre-war D-45 that Walker had bought at the same time Ernest Tubb bought his. Mac asked if he had anything else, and Walker found this clean 000-28 in his closet.

▲ Charlie Walker's 1953 Martin 000-28. It can be distinguished from its pre-war brethren by its lack of the herringbone trim found on earlier models.

▲ Two photos of Walker and his guitar, a few decades apart.

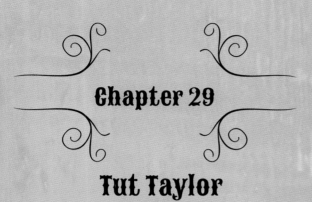

Chapter 29

Tut Taylor

From the early 1960s onward, Tut Taylor was regarded as the king of the Dobro players, with his flat-picked instrument's distinctive peal joining in with Bill Monroe, Porter Wagoner, Norman Blake, John Hartford, Roland and Clarence White, Roy Acuff, Leon Russell, and a host of other musicians who were happy to be in Taylor's company, all the more so because he was also a great storyteller.

He recorded several acclaimed solo albums and earned a Grammy for his part in 1994's *The Great Dobro Sessions* album, which he played on and coproduced with the next generation's acclaimed Dobro player, Jerry Douglas. Taylor passed away in 2015 at the age of ninety-one. He played until nearly the end of his days.

Mac first met Taylor in the early seventies, when he was a customer at Nashville's GTR guitar shop, of which Taylor was a co-owner. As most people did who entered Taylor's sphere, Mac became friends with him. Among their times together, they visited Norman Blake in Georgia. That was Taylor's idea of a good time. In contrast, when Taylor won his Grammy, Mac asked him why he didn't go to be honored at the awards ceremony, and was told, "They'll send it to me. It's not a big deal."

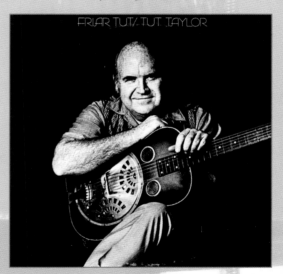

◁ Tut Taylor's 1936 Dobro, his main instrument for decades. Taylor had also worked as a sign painter, hence the personalized paint job on his case.

⚠ Tut on Norman Blake's porch.

▲ In the mid-1920s, Czechoslovakian immigrant John Dopyera developed a guitar on which the strings' bridge rested atop three cones of spun aluminum, resulting in greater volume, the lack of which was guitarists' main complaint in that era. The instrument also had a distinctive metallic tone that particularly lent itself to being played in the Hawaiian style with a metal bar on the strings. Country musicians were quick to adopt the new instruments.

These "resophonic" guitars were initially made under the National brand. In 1928 Dopyera and his brothers formed a new company, Dobro, and began producing resonator guitars with a single metal cone. Some models had metal bodies; others, like Taylor's, had wooden bodies.

Chapter 30

Norman Blake

Norman Blake is a household name, at least in the better musical households. The Tennessee native is a living repository of traditional music, be it folk, bluegrass, or any other stringed music rooted in real life, while those influences flow through his own songs to someplace new. Accomplished on guitar, mandolin, banjo, and Dobro, Blake spent a decade in Johnny Cash's band and played on Bob Dylan's *Nashville Skyline* and other timeless records, including ones by Kris Kristofferson, Joan Baez, and John Hartford. He's been heard by millions on the *O Brother, Where Art Thou?* soundtrack and on Alison Krauss and Robert Plant's *Raising Sand*.

◁ Norman Blake's 1934 Martin D-18H, which Mac photographed at a 1,200-year-old shrine in Kyoto, before a priest chased him away.

△ Blake on his porch, with wife Nancy and Tut Taylor, and with Mac behind the lens.

All of which is only supplemental to Blake's own music, most often played with his wife Nancy (on cello, guitar, mandolin, accordion, and fiddle), which is generally pristine in delivery and with an unforced emotional honesty. Blake made his first recording under his own name in 1972, and was still actively recording in 2017. The title of his 2015 album *Wood, Wire and Words*, he told an interviewer, "is basically what my life has been about since I was eleven or twelve years old."

Mac was an early fan of Blake's music, and got to know him well on trips to the Blakes' Georgia home with Tut Taylor. He got most of these instruments directly from Blake.

◁ This herringbone-bordered Dreadnought
was a favored Blake guitar for years and
has experienced so much "honest wear"
that one would hate to see what dishonest
wear looks like. Mac is of the opinion that
1934 was an exceptional year for Martins,
in terms of tone and projection, and this
example could be Exhibit A for that.

⚠ Blake's **1934** Martin Đ-18H. C.
F. Martin & Co., located in rural
Pennsylvania, could be a stodgy
outfit—company correspondence
in the **1930**s predicted electric
guitars would be a short-lived
fad—but it had been quick to
jump on the Hawaiian music
craze in the **1920**s. A good
thing, too, since ukulele
sales kept the company
afloat during the Đepression.

Martin also built Hawaiian
guitars. Since they were
played with a metal bar slid
along the strings, the action
was raised, while the frets
were ground down to a purely
ornamental height. Blake's was
converted to be played convention-
ally, and he put it to use on a noted
instructional video he made.

187

NORMAN BLAKE

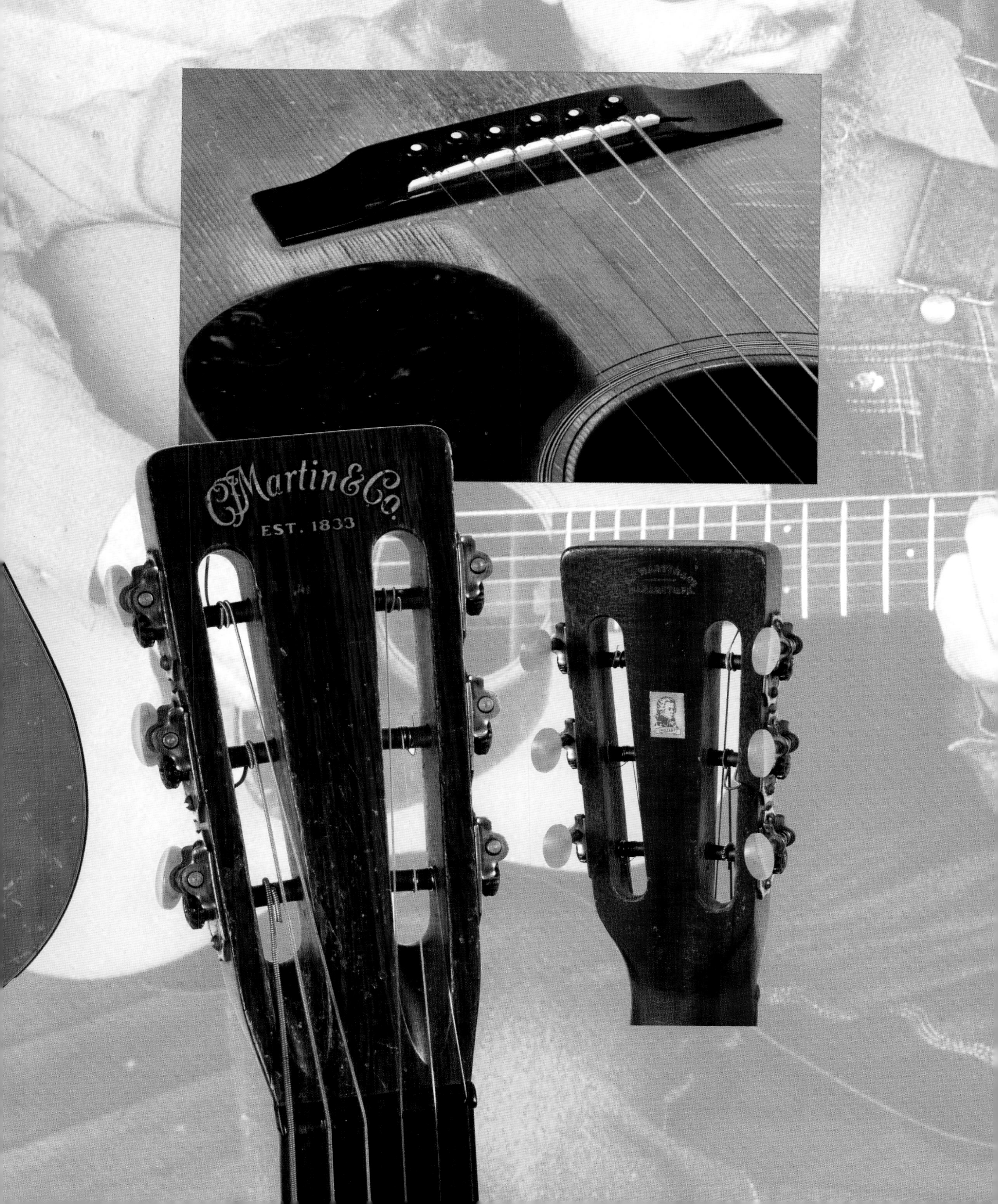

◁ Blake's Oahu guitar.
Another little stunner
of an instrument.
Oahu was a Cleveland,
Ohio-based music
publishing company
that sold instruments
made for them by
Harmony, Kay, Regal,
and other guitar com-
panies. Most Oahus
were beginner-grade
instruments, but there
were some ornate
models such as this.

NORMAN BLAKE

▽ Norman Blake's Gibson F-5 mandolin. The F-5 is widely regarded by bluegrass players and others as the pinnacle of mandolin design. It was the result of Gibson's Lloyd Loar and Guy Hart refining the violin-derived construction that Orville Gibson had applied to fretted instruments at the end of the 19th century. Introduced in 1922, the F-5 is still considered the instrument to equal nearly a hundred years later.

NORMAN BLAKE

⬜ Blake's Vega
mandolin. Just because you
have the best mandolin, doesn't
mean you can't get inspiration from
other ones. This ornate Vega mandolin
could do that on looks alone.

⬜ Blake working out on the D-28 for an as-yet-unreleased
album of Hank Snow songs Mac recorded in Nashville.

Chapter 31

David Bromberg

As both a sideman and under his own banner, multi-instrumentalist David Bromberg has had a long and storied career. In the 1960s, he divided his studies between Columbia University and the Reverend Gary Davis, who taught him his fingerpicking style. On guitar, mandolin, violin, and other stringed things, he recorded with Bob Dylan, Jerry Jeff Walker, John Hartford, John Prine, Willie Nelson, Jerry Garcia, and others. George Harrison played on Bromberg's first album. His records have been a rich mix of bluegrass, folk, blues, jazz, and rock.

He's also been influential in his choice of instruments. Bromberg was playing a Fender Broadcaster before many even knew what one was. He had his 1930s Martin F-7 archtop converted into a flattop by New York City luthier Matt Umanov, prompting such a demand for similar instruments that Martin ultimately issued a version of it.

When Bromberg wanted a Broadcaster, he was so intent on it that he travelled to Japan specifically to get Mac's, which had serial number 19.

Mac recalls, "I'd bought that Broadcaster from Gruhn for $2,750 or something. I didn't want to sell it, but Bromberg wanted it so bad I just gave it to him with the understanding that he'd send me a guitar he felt was of equal value. He sent me the F-9, which was one of the first conversions.

"Some time passed and I heard Matt Umanov had the Broadcaster. I'd only let it go because Bromberg wanted it so much, so I bought it back from Matt for $7,500. Then I sold the F-9 to George Gruhn, and then it wound up coming back to me at a guitar show."

◁ David Bromberg's 1942 Martin F-9 conversion. Originally an archtop, it is similar in shape to Martin's popular 000 size, but an inch wider, and its Brazilian rosewood back is slightly arched. Luthier Marc Silber did the first conversion of a Martin F-series archtop in the early 1960s, and Matt Umanov did the second one, which Bromberg made famous. This fancier F-9 is similar, with a new top and bracing converting it to a flattop.

△ Mac and David Bromberg giving their Martin 000-45s a playdate in Kobe, Japan, in the 1970s. The fellow on the left was Mac's high school Judo instructor, Mr. Toshiichiro Shizuka.

⚠ Two other views of Bromberg's F-9 conversion.

DAVID BROMBERG

△ Bromberg's **1938 Martin Đ-45**. For a long time, it belonged to collector Akihiko Jimbo, who had it on display at his Hotel California hotel, along with Red Smiley's Đ-45, which had a consecutive serial number with Bromberg's. For more info, see the chapter on Smiley.

Chapter 32

Ricky Skaggs

Long before "Americana" became the catchall category for roots music, the term "New Traditionalists" popped up in the 1980s, just in time for it be applied to Ricky Skaggs. Contemporary country was already sounding like seventies California pop-rock, but Skaggs was ringing the old school bell.

Before he was ten, he had been amazing audiences with his prowess on mandolin, fiddle, and guitar. At fifteen he joined bluegrass legend Ralph Stanley's Clinch Mountain Boys.

After further seasoning with the Whites and Emmylou Harris' Hot Band, Skaggs took off as a solo artist. In the 1980s, he proved there was still a market for old-time country, with hits like "Crying My Heart Out Over You," "Heartbroke," and "Don't Cheat in Our Hometown."

Skaggs has also been a traditionalist in his choice of instruments. His aged Martin D-28 guitars were the same model many of his heroes were playing in country's glory days.

Mac first saw Skaggs at a bluegrass festival in the early 1970s, when Skaggs had teamed up with Keith Whitley in a Stanley Brothers–inspired act. He later got to know Mac backstage at the Opry. Once Skaggs focused more on playing mandolin, Mac bought these Martins from him.

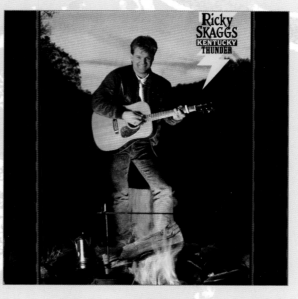

△ **Skaggs on record with his cleaner D-28.**

◁ **Ricky Skaggs' weathered 1949 Martin D-28.**

⚠ Skaggs' **1937 Martin D-28.** It looks better than Skaggs' **1949,** but it required extensive renovation to get that way.

⚠ In 1985, Skaggs confessed to *Frets* magazine, "I've let my instruments run down a little bit. I really shouldn't have done that, but I just don't have the time to look after them on the road."

Along with the wear, Skaggs installed a Takamine pickup and equalizer in the '49 D-28, which necessitated sawing out a section of the Brazilian rosewood sides. That's sacrilege in some circles, but to Skaggs it was a necessary sacrifice to get a good amplified stage and recording sound.

▷ Roy Buchanan's 1951 Fender "Nocaster." Like Karl Farr's
Fender, this guitar was made during the brief transition
period in 1951 when, for legal reasons, the name
was changed from Broadcaster to Telecaster.
The guitars made in between that change
had no name on the headstock.

⬧ Roy Buchan-
an's 1953 Fender
Telecaster. This was Buchanan's
primary guitar through many years of
his career. It was nicknamed Nancy by
him. Part of its personality comes from its
being wired a little differently than other Teles.

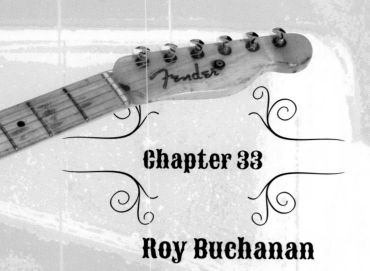

Chapter 33

Roy Buchanan

Roy Buchanan's fingers spanned a lot of musical styles over the fretboard of his 1953 Fender Telecaster: primal rockabilly with both Dale Hawkins and Ronnie Hawkins, country with Merle Kilgore, blues and R&B with Johnny Otis, and all that and more in his solo career.

Buchanan was born in Arkansas and grew up there and near Bakersfield, California, where there was no lack of hot Tele players. After years of touring as a sideman, he put down roots near Washington, DC, and settled into a local bar gig. There, plugging his Tele straight into an amp, his hands wrangled a startling range of sounds and moods from the thing. Even in that low-profile setting he became a legend, someone so many musicians told others about that the Public Broadcasting System took an interest, and aired a one-hour TV special on him.

That brought Buchanan worldwide fame, a recording career, and opportunities to play with Jeff Beck, Danny Gatton, Jerry Garcia, and other top players. His career was cut short by his untimely death in 1988 at age forty-eight.

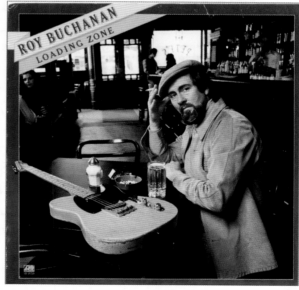

▲ Buchanan, thinking some Tele thoughts.

⚠ Details of Buchanan's "Nancy" Telecaster. That hole in the headstock? Maybe it was for hanging the guitar on a hook. Maybe it was a place to park his cigarettes.

⚠ **Other views of the "Nocaster."**

Chapter 34

J. Geils

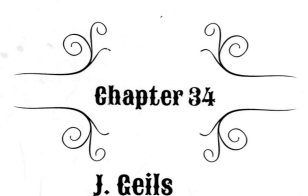

This is not a country star's guitar, but it certainly has the hallmarks of one, including mother-of-pearl binding and the artist's name inlaid in the fingerboard. The artist this time, however, was R&B/blues/rock master J. Geils. The guitar is a crazy-rare 1958 Gibson Flying V. And like many a country-star guitar, the modifications perpetrated on this instrument can make modern-day collectors hang their heads and moan.

Initially a fan of jazz, Geils got turned onto blues music while in college in the mid-1960s, and sold his car to buy his first guitar and amp. He went through a number of guitars before the Flying V became his chief stage guitar. In the early 1970s, there was virtually no information available on rare guitars. People knew Flying Vs were scarce, but no one knew how scarce, while its odd shape didn't endear it to many players. Geils traded a steel guitar and a Gibson ES-350T to get his.

Geils took it to luthier Ed Murray at Boston's Wurlitzer Music to add the abalone and rewire it. Later, Geils also had the guitar refinished ivory, covering the Korina wood body.

The J. Geils Band he formed in 1967 hit mainstream success in the early 1980s, and then broke up in 1985. In the 1990s Geils did a reversal of when he'd sold his car to get a guitar: He sold off his guitars to fund his passion for restoring Italian sports cars.

Mac was a fan of the Geils Band, so when his V with its countryish appointments turned up at a guitar show, it joined Mac's herd.

◀ J. Geils and his V
driving the J. Geils Band
at a Japanese concert.

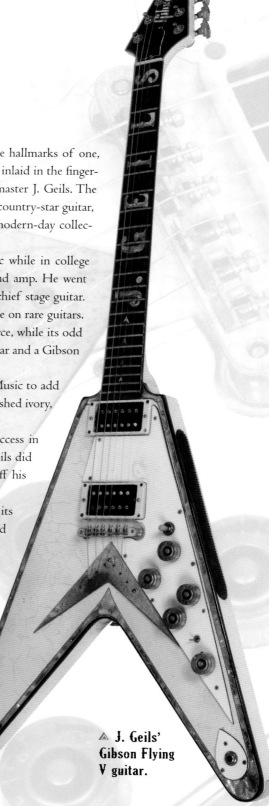

▲ J. Geils'
Gibson Flying
V guitar.

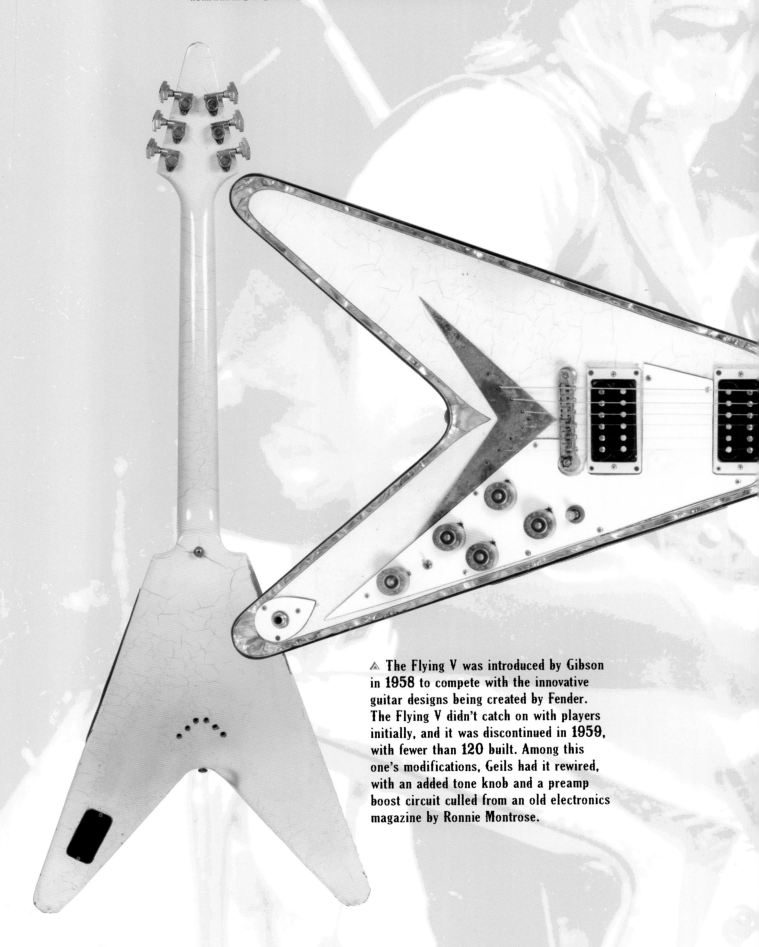

⬒ The Flying V was introduced by Gibson in 1958 to compete with the innovative guitar designs being created by Fender. The Flying V didn't catch on with players initially, and it was discontinued in 1959, with fewer than 120 built. Among this one's modifications, Geils had it rewired, with an added tone knob and a preamp boost circuit culled from an old electronics magazine by Ronnie Montrose.

Chapter 35

Mac Yasuda's Unanticipated Life

When Mac Yasuda came to the United States in 1970, there were no "vintage guitars," only used ones, with a few exceptions: Acoustic players sought a handful of venerable Martin and Gibson flattops. Rockers were learning there was a finite number of sunburst Les Pauls, though they still could be had for $800. Eric Clapton's embrace of maple-neck Stratocasters spurred a demand for them. There were no books yet documenting old guitars, and little information elsewhere.

In Japan, American guitars were so rarely seen that Mac's judo teacher was held in awe simply for owning a Gibson Everly Brothers model.

"We were all fascinated with and longing for American pop culture, mostly because after the war all Japan really had was the land and the ancient culture, but no material things," Mac recalls. "The United States had everything: cars, movies, TVs, guitars, new music. Everything we saw that offered an exciting, modern life was coming from the US."

In Mac's year of study in the US, he attended Michigan Tech by day, while at night he began earning $50 per gig in a country band. In the town library, he'd search local and distant newspapers' classifieds for guitars he could afford. His first was a 1950s Gibson ES-175 in a pawnshop for $100.

⊿ Mac singing country in Kobe, in the college band the Rodeo Rangers. Hank Snow and his band signed the guitar.

◁ Mac Yasuda at Hank Snow's house, recreating one of the cover photos for Hank Snow's *Souvenirs* album.

⊿ Mac fronting a country band in Michigan in 1971. It figures that he's the only one playing an American instrument.

"This was stuff I had dreamed about, and suddenly I was living that dream," Mac says. "Soon I had twenty guitars and wanted more."

A friend began mailing him envelopes with $1,000 cash to buy and ship guitars to Japan to resell. That inspired Mac to do likewise, and he soon opened Mac's Guitar Gallery inside a relative's store in Kobe. He sold out of American guitars quicker than he could bring them in, a feat noticed by the adjacent Yamaha music store.

Mac forgot about a career in engineering when Yamaha began handing him checks for $50,000 to find American guitars for their sixteen stores. They also had him write for their magazine. Using knowledge gleaned from George Gruhn and others on his American forays, Mac's columns almost single-handedly created an informed vintage market in Japan.

In 1984, he moved to California to represent Japan's largest herbal medicine company, with the understanding that he would be out hunting guitars several days a week. Then, and throughout subsequent wide-ranging gigs, Mac continued performing whenever he could. He wound up becoming friends with several of the musicians who had been his heroes, including Hank Snow, Porter Wagoner, and Billy Walker, and they began hosting him as a musical guest on the Grand Ole Opry.

This was a huge thing to Mac, and he admits to being scared his first time. "Of course I was: It was the Grand Ole Opry, where so many great people

had stood. But they only have you on for one song, and I figured just my wearing a Nudie suit would be enough to get me through that. And the band there is so good, they make it easy for you to be good."

He joined Opry stars on summer tours of "the corndog circuit" of Southern states' county fairs. Mac says, "That's where I really got to know some of these people. Along with Porter, there'd be Hank Locklin, Hank Thompson. Bill Anderson, Jimmy Dickens, Jack Greene, and a lot of others. We'd be stuck in one big dressing area for hours between shows, drinking, eating, and talking. I'm sure I was the oddball there. I'm walking around in a Nudie suit like them, and they're treating me as an equal, but I'm still such a big fan. If Hank Locklin was sitting with his guitar working on a new song, I was wishing I was filming it."

Mac appeared on the *Opry* dozens of times in the 1990s. Eventually, most of his friends on the show died, and the fun went out of it for him.

Throughout the years, whenever he could, he bought his heroes' worn guitars and rhinestone-besotted stage suits, some directly from them, some from their estates, or through dealers or auction houses. He also had a number of suits made. When Nudie's Rodeo Tailors closed its doors on September 29, 1994, Mac was the shop's final customer, and CNN's coverage

◁ **Mac making the rounds in Nashville, with Dolly Parton and Ernest Tubb.**

featured Mac singing a farewell to the shop.

He's the fanboy kid from another land who was welcomed into the clubhouse by his heroes, the guy dreaming of a guitar in a store window who has now owned thousands of the world's finest guitars. He's proud to have been able to preserve so much country history, and it's made him happy, but not necessarily satisfied.

"I'm always wondering what the next guitar or suit will be, or if any of the famously missing country guitars will show up, like Ernest Tubb's D-45 and Epiphone Deluxe, or Hank Snow's tooled leather cover for his D-28," he mentions, in case you have one laying around.

⚠ **Mac's pink Nudie suit with floral embroidery, 1990s. This is a copy of the suit Hank Snow wore on the Japanese issue of his *Souvenirs* album.**

⬈ Mac's white Nudie suit
with black embroidery, 1994.

⚠ Mac's purple Nudie suit, patterned after one of Porter Wagoner's suits. This is the very last suit made in Nudie's shop before it closed its doors on September 22, 1994.

⚠ This white Porter Wagoner–style suit was made by Nudie's head tailor in his later years, Manuel Ortiz, not to be confused with Manuel Cuevas, who was Nudie's right-hand man until the mid-1970s.

⚠ **Another darned Nudie suit.**

△ A red Nudie suit with gold floral embroidery,
keeping company with a custom Yasuda guitar.

▷ A fanciful suit by West Coast clothier Harvey Krantz.

⬜ Harvey Krantz made this blue suit with fabric from a Japanese kimono. More on that banjo in a moment.

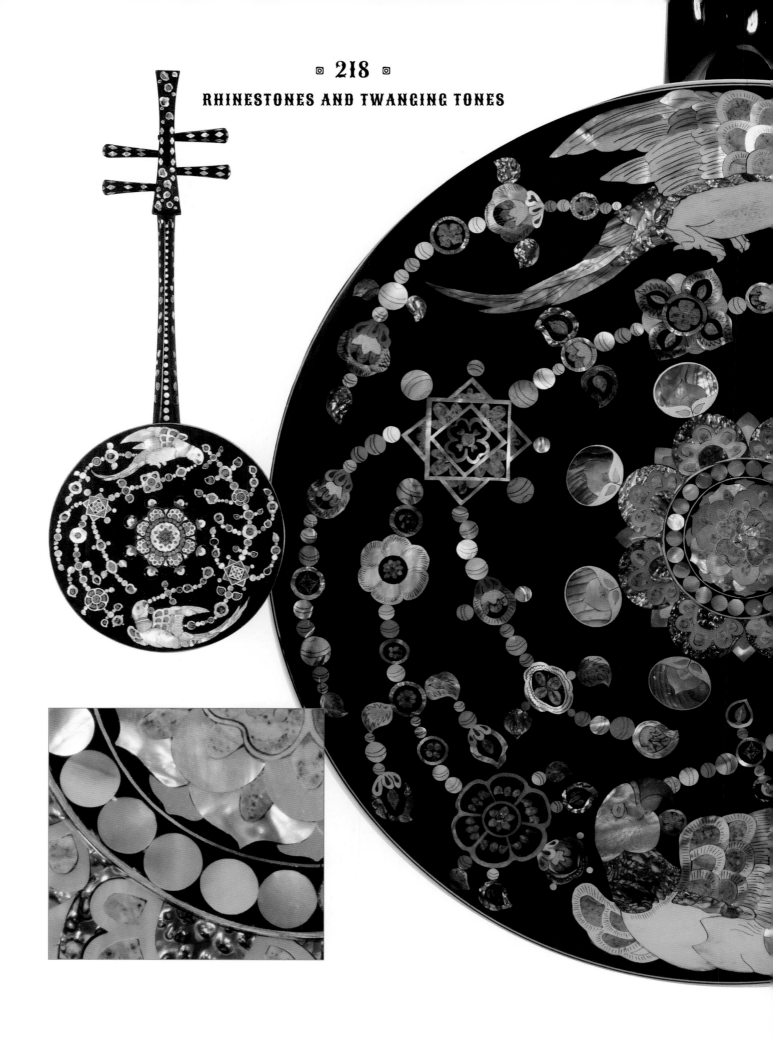

⚠ An 8th-century Biwa (upper left) that is housed in the Sho-soin Repository in Japan, and the banjo inspired by it that Mac had made by Gibson's custom shop. Acclaimed inlay artist Larry Robinson did the remarkable work on it. The accepted wisdom is that the first banjos originated in Africa in the 18th century, and Mac thought so, too, until he saw the banjo-like Biwa in the Emperor's treasure house.

▷ Even Iron Man doesn't have a silver Nudie belt.

▲ Mac had Crafters of Tennessee make deluxe custom guitars to give to several of his Opry friends. It was a show of respect to them, and also a hint that they might want to retire their old guitars and sell them to him. Here are several of the instruments arrayed on the Opry stage.

◁ Mac also had a guitar made for the king of the singing cowboys, Gene Autry. He and his wife Kimiyo presented it to Autry in his office.

⟁ Some Autry guitar details.

◁ One of the guitars Mac had made was for Del Reeves, who returned the guitar to Mac as unusable. It played and sounded fine, but Reeves received complaints from older fans who found the bikini offensive. That's Kayton Roberts of Hank Snow's Rainbow Ranch Boys standing next to Reeves.

△ Details from one of Mac's own custom J-200-influenced guitars.

⚠ Mac and his son Sotaro, bonding over a couple of old guitars. Sotaro is a popular TV and movie actor in Japan.

⚠ Steven Seagal with a guitar that once belonged to Jimi Hendrix. In 1998, Mac got a call from Marty Stuart, asking him to come to the movie set of Steven Seagal's *Fire Down Below* in the hills north of Los Angeles. Along with being able to chop or kick most things to smithereens, Seagal plays and collects guitars, and wanted to meet Mac, and use one of his D-45s in the film. They struck up an abiding friendship. Mac claims he has "a true samurai spirit," even though the characters Seagal plays haven't been able to keep Mac's character from being killed in two of his movies.

⚠ Mac with Rainbow Ranch Boys fiddler Tommy Vaden, steel guitarist Kayton Roberts, and bass player Roger Carroll, recording an album of Hank Snow songs in Nashville's venerable Hilltop studio. Snow had planned to participate, but died before he could, and Mac shelved the project. Mac did release a Hank Williams tribute album in 1996, recorded at Hilltop with surviving members of Williams' band, the Drifting Cowboys. Mac was so intent upon getting an authentic sound that they even managed to wrest Don Helms' original steel guitar from a museum for the session.

⚠ Mac performed on several Grand Ole Opry road show tours in the 1990s. Gathered backstage at a county fair in Florida are Johnny Counterfeit, Johnnie Wright, Billy Walker, Kitty Wells, Bobby Wright, Bill Anderson, Opry MC Eddie Stubbs, Jimmy C. Newman, Mac Yasuda, and Freddie Hart. If Mac's jacket looks too small, it's because he borrowed it from Hank Snow for the show.

⚠ Mac began appearing on the Grand Ole Opry in 1993, and was an old hand at it by 1995. It was still an emotional moment for him, though, when Hank Snow hosted him on the show that year.

⚠ Mac, living the "Hi" life.

Bibliography

Babiuk, Andy. *The Paul Bigsby Story*. FG Publishing, Savannah, Georgia, 2008.

Eng, Steve. *A Satisfied Mind: The Country Music Life of Porter Wagoner*. Rutledge Hill Press, Nashville, Tennessee, 1992.

George-Warren, Holly and Michelle Freedman. *How the West Was Worn*. Harry N. Abrams, Inc. New York, New York with Autry Museum of Western Heritage, Los Angeles, California, 2000.

Nudie, Jamie Lee and Mary Lynn Cabrall. *Nudie: the Rodeo Tailor*. Gibbs Smith, Salt Lake City, Utah., 2004.

O'Neal, Bill and Fred Goodwin. *The Sons of the Pioneers*. Eakin Press, Austin, Texas, 2001.

Snow, Hank with Jack Ownbey and Bob Burris. *The Hank Snow Story*. University of Illinois Press, Urbana and Chicago, Illinois, 1994.

Tosches, Nick. *Country: The Biggest Music in America*. Dell Publishing, New York, New York, 1977.

Washburn, Jim with Dick Boak. *The Martin Archives*. Hal Leonard Books, Milwaukee, Wisconsin, 2016.

About the Authors

Mac Yasuda is one of the world's foremost guitar experts and collectors, and has authored and photographed several books and countless magazine articles about them in Japan. As a singer and guitarist, he's performed numerous times on the Grand Ole Opry and other stages, and in 1996 released a CD, *Hey Good Lookin'*, of Hank Williams songs. He's been involved in numerous pursuits, including helping to produce his friend Steven Seagal's films in Asia, but his first love remains music and guitars.

Jim Washburn is the author, with Dick Boak, of *The Martin Archives*, and coauthored *Martin Guitars: An Illustrated Celebration of America's Greatest Guitarmaker* with Richard Johnston. His writing about guitars has appeared in the *Fretboard Journal* and other publications. Since 1983, he has written about popular culture, music, film, politics, and humor for the *Los Angeles Times*, the *Orange County Register*, the *OC Weekly*, the *Boston Globe*, MSN, and others. He is very much looking forward to writing some books that are free of facts and organizational skills.